Mozart

Mozart
Hugh Ottaway

Orbis Publishing

LONDON

© *Orbis Publishing Limited, London 1979*
Filmset and printed by
BAS Printers Limited, Over Wallop, Hampshire
ISBN 0 85613 069 9

Above: Mozart, the last portrait from life; silverpoint
drawing by Doris Stock, Dresden, 1789.

Endpaper: Autograph score of Piano Trio in D Minor, K. 442

Title page: Don Giovanni, Act 1, finale; coloured lithograph by
Julius Nisle, 1841, Don Giovanni confronts his enemies.

CONTENTS

PREFACE

When invited to write this book, I was urged to keep in mind the needs of the general reader who has been 'caught' by Mozart's music but is not familiar with musical terminology. This I have tried to do, not with the intention of 'writing down', but rather with a view to re-examining technical terms whenever they insisted on being used. And insist they did! They always will, if only because music is a 'non-representational' art. Sometimes such terms are explained as they arise, but often this method would have broken the continuity unduly—hence the need for a glossary. Music examples have been kept to a minimum; they are resorted to only in those places in the text where close attention to musical detail simply cries out for them. I believe that notation, carefully used, is capable of helping even those who say that they 'can't read music'; for instance, *Ex. 14*, which is the most elaborate, will convey its essential point to anyone with an eye for recurring shapes.

What I have attempted to do is to present a much romanticized life-story *unromantically*, but without detracting from the phenomenon that is Mozart's creativity. Indeed, such human weaknesses and foibles as emerge should enhance, not diminish, one's awareness of that phenomenon. I hope this is realism, and that people, places and the historical setting have been treated in a realistic manner. At the same time, both in the text and in some of the pictures, the sentimental tradition has been recognized—rather in the spirit of 'know your enemy'.

For factual detail I have turned to the usual sources—Anderson, Deutsch, Einstein, Schenk, etc. (see Bibliography)—and also to some earlier and more recent ones. The prevailing pattern is chronological with life and works considered together. In Chapter 9, however, the pattern is broken by a discussion of the later piano concertos and the string quintets, and Chapter 12, 'Mozart and Ourselves', is in the nature of an epilogue. This last is concerned with changing attitudes to Mozart: not a history of Mozart in performance and in scholarship—that would require another volume—but a reflection of some of the principal viewpoints.

Two matters of substance remain to be dealt with. The first of these is the sonata principle, which represents a new conception of musical structure and expression fundamental to the Classical style and therefore to Mozart. For general discussion, the term sonata *principle*, or outlook, is preferable to sonata *form*. The latter may well suggest something too rigid—a mould for casting, or a structural blueprint—a notion readily confirmed by many textbook and popular descriptions, which tend to give too much emphasis to contrasting themes.

The essential quality has more to do with tonality (key) than with themes: the way in which a key is established, undermined and supplanted. But first, the term itself: the fact that we say *sonata* principle, rather than symphonic or quartet principle, is due to the important role of sonatas for keyboard instruments in fashioning the new outlook. The term is unfortunate in suggesting something peculiar to sonatas, for what it signifies is common to all the Classical instrumental genres and is also a powerful force in opera and in choral music. This is best thought of as an approach to musical structure and expression based on a dramatic exploitation of key.

One of the most important aspects, and yet the least written about, is the quality of movement that makes the tonal drama a reality; such metaphors as athleticism and muscular activity may be helpful here. For one of the marvels of the Classical style is the way in which its characteristic energy seems to be generated within the music itself, determining the shape, direction and intensity as if the composition were a living organism.

This organic illusion will be sustained by every fine performance of a good Classical work, and nowhere more so than in those passages where 'development' occurs. Development consists of two things: (i) an intensification of the tonal activity, which is defined by (ii) a close working of some salient feature (motive) from the thematic material. This is by no means confined to the so-called development section of a sonata form. In the later works of Mozart, as in those of Haydn, another likely place is towards the middle of the recapitulation: see, for example, the first movement of the Symphony No. 40 in G minor (K. 550), bars 200–210, and the finale of the *Jupiter* Symphony (K. 551), bars 233–53. The more mature and complex a Classical sonata form, the more pervasive is developmental writing likely to be. Nevertheless, the textbook three-part plan—exposition, development and recapitulation—is sound enough:

Exposition. The tonic key (home key) is established and thematically defined.

The theme is described as the 'first subject'; if there is more than one theme at this stage, 'first group' is preferable. In a so-called bridge, or transition, which may well be a modulating (key-changing) counter-statement of the first subject, the music pulls away from the tonic key and towards a related key. The new key is usually that of the dominant (the fifth degree of the scale; for example, the dominant of C is G), or, if the movement has begun in a minor key, the relative major. Whatever the new key, it is established in a way that, for the time being, gives it an ascendancy over the tonic key. It is defined thematically by a second subject/group, which may well be followed by a distinctive 'closing theme' in the same key.

Development. Although often described as a working-out of the themes, this is primarily concerned with tonal drama—an exploration of more or less remote keys. All or none of the themes from the exposition may be used. Sometimes new material is introduced; frequently one or two short motives from the themes bear the weight of the argument.

Recapitulation. Ideally, a re-creation of the exposition in the light of the development. The tonal drama is resolved; both subjects/groups are restated in the tonic key. But there is still scope for key-tension; the rewriting of the transition so that the music moves away from the tonic key only to return may be dramatically exploited in the manner of the development.

This generalization is concerned with the barest of bare bones—with basic structure, that is to say; it takes no account of the expressive contrasts, tensions and surprises that give flesh to the bones in so many ways. In the Classical sonata style, however, structure and expression are ultimately inseparable; even the smallest expressive details may be felt as a function of that muscular activity which animates the whole.

In broad cultural terms, this dynamic conception in which tensions are generated, developed and ultimately resolved is the characteristic musical creation of the Enlightenment. The social setting in which it evolved was to a large extent aristocratic, but, significantly, it was not at Versailles, Potsdam or even Schönbrunn—the principal courts of the old order—that the crucial developments took place. Our attention is drawn to some of the lesser courts— at Mannheim, for example—and to some of the more thriving cities. There we find a coming-together of progressive-minded aristocrats and middle-class thinkers and artists seeking a more liberal culture: a fraternization characteristic of the whole of the Enlightenment. Such men could meet on terms of equality in their own private circles—Mozart's relationship in Vienna with Count Cobenzl, Baron van Swieten and others is typical—and in that institution which, more than any other, represents the ideals of the Enlightenment: freemasonry.

In the 1780s many musicians were freemasons, but none more ardently than Mozart. Since to most of us today the word masonic means either 'good works' or business graft, a brief introductory note seems desirable. In its eighteenth-century form, freemasonry was founded in England and developed extensively throughout Europe. From the outset, the Catholic Church was strongly antagonistic, as were many kings and princes. For example, that same Duke Karl Theodor, Elector Palatine, who at Mannheim encouraged his musicians to innovate, was one of those who banned masonry; in the 1780s, when he was also Elector of Bavaria, he actively persecuted the Illuminati, the masonic left wing in the German lands. The significance of the fact that eighteenth-century autocrats, both secular and ecclesiastical, saw in masonry a threat to their authority goes far beyond the secrecy with which the order conducted itself. The emphasis on reason, virtue and human brotherhood, the practice of natural religion and ethical humanism, these constituted an advanced liberal ideology which even 'enlightened' rulers tended to view with anxiety. The widespread belief, fostered by propagandists of the *ancien régime*, especially in Vienna, that the freemasons were responsible for the French Revolution is the kind of fiction that would make history a great deal tidier, if only it were true. There is, of course, a sense in which it 'ought' to have been true, for masonry was indeed a seedbed for liberal and democratic ideas.

SALZBURG AND THE
MOZART FAMILY

Those who love Salzburg will tell you that nowhere else are music, landscape and architecture so magically blended. And there is much truth in that. If Mozart had not been born there, some other excuse for festive music-making would have had to be found.

Salzburg today owes much of its fame and not a little of its fortune to the Mozart connection. There is an air of prosperity, a prosperity inseparable from the wealthier kind of tourism, which effectively began with the founding of the Festival after World War I. Before that, for about a century, Salzburg had been a sleepy provincial town, haunted by a past that was scenically and architecturally inescapable, but becoming more dilapidated with each decade. Only since the defeat of Napoleon in 1815 had the town and the province been a part of Austria and of the Habsburg Empire. In the eighteenth century, Salzburg counted for something in its own right. Ruled by independent prince-archbishops with a nominal allegiance to the Holy Roman Emperor, it was large enough to sustain a sizable if poorly paid administration, and small enough to keep out of much dynastic conflict.

The last prince-archbishop was Count Hieronymus Colloredo (1772–1803), whom posterity has not yet forgiven for dismissing Mozart from his service. Indeed, some find satisfaction in noting that Colloredo was himself removed by Napoleon, who handed Salzburg to neighbouring Bavaria. History, however, does well to avoid too keen a sense of poetic justice. As we shall see, Colloredo was very much a man of his age, a minor exponent of 'enlightened despotism', and a more worthy ruler than many of his contemporaries. Interestingly, posterity

The Italianate façade of the *Mozarts Geburtshaus* (birthplace), now Getreidegasse 9. The third floor was the home of the Mozart family from 1747 until 1773. All seven children of Leopold and Anna Maria were born in this house.

11

Salzburg in the eighteenth
century: the Kollegienkirche, or
University Church, in 1735. An
engraving by Carl Remshard
(1678–1735) from a drawing by
Franz Anton Daureiter
(1695–1760).

takes a gentler view of the most illustrious of his predecessors, Wolf
Dietrich (1587–1612) and Markus Sittikus (1612–19), two cultivated
voluptuaries who laid the foundations of the new, Baroque Salzburg
within the walls of the medieval city.

In the earlier stages, and especially in the building of the cathedral,
Italian influence was strong: Salzburg, after all, is only just north of the
Alps. But the typically Austrian and Bavarian version of Baroque came
to prevail. It was in Salzburg that Fischer von Erlach perfected his
architectural skills before moving on to Vienna: see, for instance, the
Kollegienkirche (University Church) and the Dreifaltigkeitskirche
(Holy Trinity Church), the one behind the Getreidegasse, the other at
the top of the Makartplatz. Something of a medieval presence
remained—in the Festung (fortress) on the Mönchsberg, immediately
above the town, in the darkly Gothic Franciscan Church, and across the
river in the Steingasse—but almost everywhere Baroque façades
appeared, even though the streets might still be narrow.

Given a sense of history and some imagination, it is not difficult to step
back into eighteenth-century Salzburg. For one thing, so much of it has
been well preserved: carefully controlled restoration, not the havoc of
developers, is the order of the day. And most of it is concentrated in the

12

very small space between the Mönchsberg and the river Salzach. An aerial picture shows clearly how concentration is reconciled with squares and courtyards; likewise the extent to which an earlier street plan remains even now. For the visitor, there is no better stimulus to the imagination than the panoramic view from the roof café of the Hotel Stein. Looking across the Salzach towards the Festung with the Untersberg beyond, one sees an array of domes and cupolas that has changed hardly at all since Mozart's time; and at sundown, the fancy that architecture is 'frozen music' becomes an almost audible truth.

A sense of reality, however, insists on two important points, the first of which is well documented: that Mozart found life in Salzburg irksome and frustrating, both musically and socially. The second point, though speculative, is closely related: the probability that Salzburg today is in almost every respect a better place to grow up in than it was two centuries ago. Then it was physically unhygienic, morally and intellectually priest-ridden, and socially claustrophobic as only a small town with a well-defined hierarchical order can be. The object of most of the more enterprising burghers was necessarily to seek some court connection, either in the way of trade, or in pursuit of an office or employment for themselves or their sons. This made for servility,

Salzburg today: the old town, showing the castle and some of the domes and cupolas. From left to right: the 'new' Residenz, Nonnberg Church, Cathedral, University Church, Franciscan Church (tower with spire) and St Peter's Church.

intrigue and back-biting and deepened the dependence of the town on the princely household and administration. From their letters, one can see the Mozarts, father and son, caught up in this web, but at the same time scorning those who made it so, and holding hard to their own self-esteem. If the scorn seems more open in Wolfgang than in his father, the reason is to be found in a difference of generation rather than of basic response. There is no doubt that Wolfgang got his self-esteem from his father, and that Leopold inculcated it from early childhood. Look at Leopold's portrait—the anonymous one (*c.* 1765) attributed to Lorenzoni: of all the portraits of eighteenth-century musicians, it is one of the most revealing.

But this is to run ahead a little. The point to be made here is that in looking out from that hotel roof, or in listening to Mozart serenades in an open courtyard of a summer evening, or simply in walking about the town before the daily influx, we are getting the best of both worlds. Our period nostalgia, as so often, is to a large extent misplaced; only when directed to that enviable composure and control which we unthinkingly call 'Classical', is it fit to be indulged.

In the Mozart story, Salzburg is approached from Augsburg, which lies beyond Munich to the north-west. It is no great distance and the brighter boys at the Jesuit schools in Augsburg were sent to the Benedictine university at Salzburg to continue their education. Leopold Mozart (1719–87) was one such. He came from a family of master masons, but his father was a successful bookbinder. His education was broadly based, extending into the sciences as well as the arts, and he took it seriously. Indeed, serious-mindedness was a fundamental trait, closely allied to the self-esteem already noted; together these fostered a sense of ambition that was necessarily social as well as intellectual. A skill in using opportunities—he would have made an excellent diplomat—is also evident at an early stage. Very probably he got to the university by letting it be thought that he would enter the priesthood, though his intentions were otherwise.

Singing and organ- and violin-playing were among Leopold's school accomplishments, and it is likely that, once at Salzburg, he found increasing scope for practising and developing such talents. When we learn that in his second year at the university he failed to attend classes and was perhaps sent down, we should suspect neither debauchery nor 'dark night of the soul'. That young man of 19 or 20 knew very well what he was about and was already making the first moves in a musical career. He became a chamber musician in the household of Count Johann of Thurn and Taxis, the senior canon of Salzburg, with whom he remained for three years. The logical next step was then taken, and he joined the first violins in the *Kapelle* (musical establishment) of the prince-archbishop himself.

Clearly, Leopold Mozart's success was due to a combination of practical musicianship, personality—well disposed to please, yet sober and dignified—and compositional prowess. He had already written a good deal of serviceable occasional music, as well as trio sonatas, church music and music for the theatre, and had given satisfaction and pleasure.

Sigismund Christoph von Schrattenbach, Prince-Archbishop of Salzburg, 1753–71; engraving by Joseph and Johann Klauber, *c.* 1760. His tolerance of Leopold Mozart's 'absenteeism' made possible Wolfgang's boyhood travels.

To us he is a minor composer, chiefly remembered for the *Toy Symphony*—formerly attributed to Haydn—and for a *Musical Sleighride* which is not in fact his; but in the Salzburg of the 1750s and 1760s, his flair for the stylistic *mot juste* and his all-round technical competence must have made him an attractive figure. Particularly successful were his south German genre-pieces such as *The Peasant Wedding*. In the mid-1750s he was given the status of 'court composer', and when the *Kapellmeister* (director of music), Johann Ernst Eberlin, died in 1762, Leopold hoped to succeed him; hoped and expected, for his relations with Eberlin had been good, and he was well thought of by the prince-archbishop, Count Sigismund Schrattenbach (1753–71). Schrattenbach's decision, however, was to promote his vice-*Kapellmeister*, Giuseppe Francesco Lolli, and to make Leopold the new deputy.

Leopold Mozart (c. 1765) and his wife, Anna Maria (c. 1775); oil paintings by an unknown Salzburg artist thought to have been Pietro Antonio Lorenzoni. The book represents Leopold's *Violinschule*.

We do not know what lay behind Lolli's appointment. Neither intrigue nor a common bias towards Italian musicians can be ruled out. On the other hand, the reputedly easy-going Schrattenbach may simply have treated the promotion as administrative routine. He was, however, fond of music, and certainly no fool, so it is possible that he had noted Leopold's reserve with the other musicians, his sense of moral and intellectual superiority, and had concluded that with such a man in charge, the *Kapelle* might well become strife-ridden. Moreover, Leopold's urge to travel had already shown itself: the first expedition with his two children—to the electoral court at Munich—dates from the beginning of the same year (1762), and at the time of Eberlin's death the Mozarts were in Vienna. Whatever the truth about the appointment may be, the effect on Leopold was profound; it was also lasting, for he remained vice-*Kapellmeister* to the end of his days. His mistrust of other musicians, and especially of Italians, was strengthened. (In the German lands, as elsewhere, Italian or Italian-trained musicians held many of the

best posts.) Leopold's sense of frustration went very deep: not only did he know his worth as a musician and man of culture, but since the publication, in Augsburg, of his *Versuch einer gründlichen Violinschule* (Essay on a thorough violin method) he had been recognized internationally. This wider reputation came from his book, not his music; but it was real, and among the Salzburg musicians only Michael Haydn—Joseph's younger brother, appointed to the *Kapelle* in 1762—could outstrip or even equal it. Appropriately, the *Versuch* was published in 1756, the very year in which Wolfgang was born; for Leopold's frustration has an important bearing on what he did with the child prodigy that he had fathered, and on the closeness with which he tried to direct Wolfgang's subsequent career. Throughout the next 25 years, this will remain relevant background.

First, however, we must turn to Wolfgang's mother—Anna Maria, born Pertl, the daughter of a poorly paid revenue official. Born at nearby St Gilgen, on Lake St Wolfgang, in 1720, she came to Salzburg with her

widowed mother in 1742, and there she met Leopold. Among her primary qualities were good looks, warm-heartedness and intelligence, but she was not well educated. Whenever she comes to life for us, she does so sympathetically; clearly, it was from her side of the family that Wolfgang got his sense of fun and his sunny nature. Leopold and Anna Maria were married, in the cathedral, in 1747, and made their home at what is now the celebrated *Mozarts Geburtshaus*: No. 9 Getreidegasse, a sizable, solid house owned by the wholesale grocer, Johann Hagenauer, who became a good friend. The Mozarts occupied the third floor and, despite somewhat cramped accommodation, must have thought themselves well set up. The Getreidegasse is one of the oldest, and narrowest, streets of the old town, but in those days No. 9 with its Italianate façade looked out on to a pleasant little square with a fountain. Perhaps the house was unhealthy. The back of it, at least, was medieval, and many have noticed in the entrance hall 'a smell that makes one think of drains and cats and dinners all in one, without being exactly redolent of any of these things'.[1]

The marriage was a happy one, seemingly free from serious dissension. Anna Maria deferred to Leopold on all major matters and evidently was well content with her home and children. The first three children died in early infancy. Then in 1751 Maria Anna Walburga, known as Nannerl, was born. She was not only to survive; she grew to be as talented a sister and youthful companion as any artistic prodigy could reasonably wish for. In the next few years, two more babies died. Finally, for there were no further children, on 27 January 1756, Wolfgang Amadeus was born. The baptismal register of the cathedral tells us that the hour was eight in the evening, which, unless we happen to be astrologers, is of interest only in relation to the time of baptism: ten o'clock the following morning. It was the middle of winter, the chances of survival were not good, and Leopold and Anna Maria, true to their Catholic faith, were anxious to avoid the infant soul's slipping into perdition. Perhaps they had been caught before by that pernicious doctrine, and had suffered. Either way, this is one of those moments that offer insight into the physical and spiritual realities of the age.

The survival of only two out of seven was not exceptionally poor, even for an urban middle-class family. There is nothing to suggest that the Mozarts felt hard hit; if they had done so, their acceptance of a divine providence would surely have prevailed. Besides, they soon had plenty to satisfy their parental aspirations, for both children developed early and proved remarkably responsive to tuition. From start to finish, Leopold himself took responsibility for their education. Here it is worth noting that he would have made a very successful schoolmaster; he had the

The Paris Lodron Palace, Salzburg, residence of Count Lodron, the Salzburg Marshal; oil painting by Johann Michael Sattler (1786–1847). The dome is that of Holy Trinity Church, above the Hannibalplatz (see p. 60). Mozart wrote *divertimenti* and a concerto for three pianos for the Countess and her family.

19

scholarship, the sense of purpose, and the capacity for stimulating not only interest but sustained application. His discipline may be taken for granted, for everything we know about him points to that. With Nannerl and Wolfgang he may well have been over-zealous, even oppressive, in his keenness to turn every happening to educational account; but if so, there is nowhere a hint that the children were resistant. Perhaps the secret was in starting them young. Certainly Wolfgang became involved at the earliest possible age through the lessons given to his sister.

Both children showed a ready aptitude for music. When only three, we are told, Wolfgang began putting notes together at the keyboard, and a little later he learnt to play simple pieces, faultlessly from memory, and then to invent such pieces, which his father wrote down. And possibly corrected? Of course; order and correctness were indispensable to progress. To believe that Leopold did not assist with the early compositions is as foolish as to suggest that he dictated them. Neither view is realistic, and realism is much needed here. Sentimentalists who depict the young boy as a kind of cherub-genius, like one of those Rococo baby-faces in an Austrian church brought to life by St Cecilia herself, can very easily lead us astray.

The sentimental tradition is an old one, reaching back to the Mozart family circle. Leopold, however, was sufficiently hard-headed, though capable of being deeply moved by his son's more improbable feats. An incident recalled by the Salzburg trumpeter and violinist, Andreas Schachtner, gives an insight into both these aspects of Leopold, as well as into Wolfgang's extraordinary musical precociousness. Writing to Nannerl after her brother's death, he told of an occasion when Leopold, himself and a third musician were sight-reading some trios. Wolfgang, who was just seven, was keen to play second violin:

> Your Papa would not let him, for he had not yet had any lessons in violin-playing, and Papa thought that he could not possibly achieve anything. Wolfgang said: 'You don't need lessons in order to play second violin.' When your Papa insisted that he should go away and stop bothering us, Wolfgang began to cry bitterly and went off moodily with his little violin. I suggested that he should be permitted to play alongside me. Eventually Papa said: 'Play with Herr Schachtner, but so softly that you can't be heard; otherwise you'll have to go.' And that is what we did.... To my surprise, I soon saw that I was not needed. Without any fuss, I put down my violin and observed your Papa; tears of wonder

and delight were running down his cheeks. In this way all six trios were played. At the end, Wolfgang was so heartened by our applause that he said he could tackle the first violin part. Just for fun, we let him try. The result was such a display of incorrect fingering that we nearly died of laughter, but he held his part.

That, one may say, is an old man's account of something that had happened 30 years before. True, it does seem odd that Leopold, of all people, had not begun to teach his seven-year-old son the violin. Nonetheless, it is clear that a remarkable feat did occur.

Another of Schachtner's memories is worth recalling for its insights into both father and son. Wolfgang, who is said to have been only four or five at the time, was busy composing a 'concerto for the clavier':

Your Papa took it from him and showed me a confusion of notes, mostly written over ink-blots. . . . At first we laughed at this bit of nonsense, but then Papa began to look into it. For quite a time he examined the notation, and then tears of joy and satisfaction fell from his eyes. 'Look, Herr Schachtner,' he said, 'see how correctly this has been done; but it couldn't be used, for it's much too difficult for anyone to play.' Wolfgang at once broke in: 'That's why it's a concerto; you must practise hard until you've got it right. Look, this is how it should go.' He played, and succeeded well enough for us to see what he wanted.

What that shows us of Wolfgang is a young boy's capacity for imitation, on a scale that amounts to virtuosity. In both these anecdotes the self-confident vigour presupposes an unusual degree of observation and receptiveness, an active receptiveness that insists on doing. This is a key not only to the boy but also to the youth; properly used, it should unlock our understanding of that prodigious talent which some indulgently confuse with genius, and should help us to avoid such confusion. Even Mozart had first to master his talent! This boyhood faculty of active receptiveness was not confined to musical pursuits; it can be seen in the flair for languages, Italian especially, and in a well-authenticated excellence at arithmetic.

We are told that Wolfgang was a highly sensitive child, even to the point of being morbidly affectionate. 'He would ask those he loved a dozen times a day whether they returned his feelings and burst into tears on being teasingly answered in the negative.' The words are Blom's,[2] but the statement is to be found in every biography. True or false? No one can be sure. All that can be said is that such hypersensitivity seems implicit in the mature music. In the childhood letters, however, it is not to be found: 'I kiss you a thousand times' and 'I remain, true till death'— both of these to Nannerl—are purely conventional. The letters have an extrovert liveliness, often a sense of fun and, most of all, acute observation combined with a quick-sure judgment.

For healthy extroversion, this short letter home, written in Milan on 30 November 1771, would be hard to beat (the writer was in his sixteenth year):

> Lest you should think I am unwell I am sending you these few
> lines. I kiss Mama's hand. My greetings to all our good friends.
> I have seen four rascals hanged here in the Piazza del Duomo.
> They hang them just as they do in Lyons.
> Wolfgang[3]

Nor is there any burden of hypersensitivity in such letters as this one, written to Nannerl about a month earlier:

> Praise and thanks be to God, I too am well. As my work is now
> finished, I have more time to write letters. But I have nothing
> to say, for Papa has told you everything already. I have no
> news except that numbers 35, 59, 60, 61, 62 were drawn in the
> lottery; and so, if we had taken these numbers, we should have
> won. But as we did not take any tickets, we have neither won
> nor lost, but we have had our laugh at other people who did.
> The two arias which were encored in the serenata were sung
> by Manzuoli and by the *prima donna*, Girelli, respectively. . . .

After all the reportage that has come down to us, it is somehow reassuring to find such ordinariness. The main trouble with the reportage is that so much of it presents the boy Wolfgang as a breath-taking wonderchild in an adult world. It is not surprising that a rounded picture is difficult to build up. From the letters, however, it is possible to imagine a boy with other boys, though one whose irrepressible bumptiousness ought to have brought him many a bloody nose—and would have done so had he gone to school. Imagination is certainly needed, for hardly ever do we actually see him with other boys. His relationship with his sister was uncommonly good, but Nannerl was four and a half years older and herself remarkably talented. Even then, his letters to her often give the impression of an elder brother: for instance, the one dated 26 January

1770—the day before his fourteenth birthday—in which he pulls her leg about having made Herr von Mölk, who was in love with Nannerl, 'sigh and suffer so frightfully'.

Whatever approach we may choose to make, it is the boy's precociousness that looms largest. In that same letter of 26 January there is a striking example of his acute assessment of other musicians. But for the cocky, boyish tone, this might be the writing of a very experienced hand; and behind it is an unquestioned authority, a confidence that never falters. An imitation of Leopold, is it? To some extent yes; but is there really any doubt that the judgments are his own? Most precocious of all is the critical detachment:

> The opera at Mantua was charming. They played [Hasse's] *Demetrio*. The *prima donna* sings well, but very softly; and when you do not see her acting, but only singing, you would think she is not singing at all. For she cannot open her mouth, but whines out everything. However, we are accustomed to that now. The *seconda donna* looks like a grenadier and has a powerful voice too, and, I must say, does not sing badly, seeing that she is acting for the first time. The *primo uomo, il musico*, sings beautifully, though his voice is uneven. His name is Caselli. . . . As for the tenors, one is called Otini. He does not sing badly, but rather heavily like all Italian tenors, and he is a great friend of ours. I do not know the name of the other one. He is still young, but not particularly good. *Primo ballerino*— good. *Prima ballerina*—good, and it is said that she is not hideous, but I have not seen her close to. The rest are quite ordinary. A *grotesco* was there who jumps well, but cannot write as I do, I mean, as sows piddle. The orchestra was not bad. In Cremona it is good. . . .

And so on, with apparent spontaneity and clarity of recollection. If you find it irritating, pause to reflect that the writer had composed two operas—*Bastien und Bastienne* and *La finta semplice*—three masses, some twelve symphonies and twenty sonatas of various descriptions, to say nothing of sundry arias and minuets, and had himself given exhibition performances all over Europe, from Vienna to London. The confidence was by no means spurious, and what Salzburg had to offer must already have seemed somewhat limited.

THE CHILD
PRODIGY

It was as a player of keyboard instruments that the boy Mozart was first launched upon the European scene. He was only six at the time, and from then until the age of 15 the exhibition tours planned by his father were the centre of his life. Between January 1762 and March 1771 only about two and a half years were spent in Salzburg, the longest period being of some ten months. Moreover, much of the time at home involved preparation for the next departure, for Leopold Mozart was certainly thorough. We shall have to look further at Leopold's motivation, and to examine both the immediate and long-term effects on Wolfgang himself. These considerations will develop naturally from an account of the main events.

Up until the Italian tour of 1769 to 1771, when father and son went on their own, the whole family travelled, and the musical precociousness of Nannerl was a part of the performance. It is worth noting that Nannerl, too, was a remarkably gifted keyboard player, and that in the middle sixties it was of Leopold Mozart and his children that people talked. Had Nannerl continued to receive the concentrated attention that Leopold lavished on Wolfgang, she could hardly have failed to make a name for herself. As she grew up, however, she seems to have been content to leave the public scene to the greater gifts of her brother. In this, no doubt, personal temperament and sisterly affection were strongly reinforced by social convention.

Munich, the Bavarian capital, was the obvious choice for a first exploratory visit. Early in 1762 the Mozarts spent three weeks there: beyond the fact that the children played before the Elector Maximilian

Leopold Mozart with Wolfgang and Nannerl in Paris, 1763/4; lithograph by Schiefendecker, after a watercolour by Louis Carmontelle. This picture was widely distributed by Leopold as an advertisement.

Joseph, and that Leopold was encouraged by the response, nothing is known of this venture. Nor is it clear with what financial resources the subsequent journeys were undertaken. Was each tour self-financing? Those who stress the profit motive should bear in mind the considerable outlay. Whatever illusions he may have had to begin with, Leopold soon discovered that the monetary rewards were unpredictable and bore no simple relationship to expressions of wonder. It is also noteworthy that, at first, the Mozarts did not have their own transport. They seem to have taken for granted the problems, hazards and discomforts of eighteenth-century travel, but just occasionally we are given a glimpse of the harsher realities.

By September 1762 Leopold was ready to present his children in Vienna and at the court of the Habsburgs. Again he had no difficulty in obtaining leave. (Archbishop Schrattenbach's lasting indulgence is usually attributed to 'reflected glory', but there is little evidence of any personal interest in the fortunes of the Mozarts.) The journey was probably made by river, for it took in Passau, where the Salzach joins the Danube, and then Linz. At both these places important contacts were made. The newly appointed Bishop of Passau, for whom Wolfgang played, was the influential Count Joseph Thun-Hohenstein, who hoped to become Schrattenbach's successor at Salzburg. Clearly, Leopold was well pleased, despite a delay of five days and the reward of only one ducat. At Linz, under the patronage of Count Leopold Schlick, Wolfgang and Nannerl gave a concert at which they won the admiration of the young Count Pálffy, who was very well connected in Vienna. Travelling ahead of the Mozarts, Count Pálffy and others enthusiastically prepared the way; Count Schlick undertook to gain the support of Count Durazzo, who controlled the musical establishment at the Habsburg court, and it only remained for Leopold to time his family's arrival to the best advantage.

Even at this stage one can see that Leopold's success depended on two things: thorough preparation and a skilful use of the unexpected. Implicit in both was a keen awareness of aristocratic connections with their 'wheels within wheels': hardly ever did a door remain closed for lack of access to the right man to open it. Just a week after reaching Vienna, the Mozarts appeared before the imperial family at Schönbrunn, with obvious success. The account that has come down to us depicts the six-year-old Wolfgang at his most exuberant, delighting the Emperor Franz I with tricks at the keyboard, jumping into the lap of the Empress Maria Theresa, whom he kissed 'good and thoroughly', and offering himself in marriage to the Archduchess Maria Antonia (the future Marie Antoinette, Queen of France), who was of the same age. When about to

Nannerl in the 'gala costume' presented by the Empress Maria Theresa; oil painting, probably by Pietro Antonio Lorenzoni, Salzburg, 1763. The head is presumably from life, but the body and background are conventional.

play a work by Georg Wagenseil, he asked for the composer himself, saying '*He* understands'. Wagenseil came to him and was invited to turn the pages.

From one point of view, this three-hour visit to Schönbrunn was brilliantly stage-managed show business; but to leave it at that is to fail to perceive how readily, and completely, the young Mozart had entered into the role assigned to him. Shyness is impossible to detect. Self-awareness and a sense of enjoyment are clearly evident: these, no less than Leopold's qualities, were indispensable to success.

A crowded programme followed. Two days later the imperial paymaster brought a gift of gala costumes for Nannerl and Wolfgang— to be seen in two portraits by an unknown artist, now in the *Mozarts Geburtshaus* (birthplace)—and on that same day no fewer than four performing visits were made to various notabilities, among them the imperial chancellor, Count Wenzel Kaunitz-Rietberg. And so it continued, with concerts as well as private visits, until Wolfgang became ill with what was mistakenly diagnosed as scarlet fever. For about a week he was very ill, and visits were in abeyance until early in November, by which time the social season had begun and there was competition from other attractions. Leopold calculated that the interruption had lost him at least 50 ducats, but he paid cheerfully for Masses in Salzburg as a thank-offering for his son's recovery.

If the Mozart children were no longer the centre of aristocratic attention, they were not forgotten. There was a further payment of 100 ducats from the imperial purse and a cordial invitation to remain longer in Vienna. On St Cecilia's day (22 November) the Mozarts dined with the court *Kapellmeister*, Georg Reutter, remembered by posterity for his dismissal of Haydn from the choir of St Stephen's in 1749. Most important of all was a visit to the French ambassador, for out of this came the invitation to Versailles that decided Leopold on a grand tour in 1763. Indeed, the idea soon became an obsession and almost certainly influenced the purchase of a 'very well suspended carriage', the immediate object of which was the hard winter journey back from Pressburg (Bratislava) to Vienna. The Mozarts had gone to Pressburg at the invitation of the Pálffy family and of other Hungarian nobles, and had found it decidedly worth their while. They were back in Vienna in time for Christmas, and Nannerl and Wolfgang made one or two further appearances. Count Durazzo's proposal of a public concert, however, was not taken up: a clear indication, surely, that plenty of money had already been made. Besides, the return to Salzburg was overdue, Leopold having extended his leave without permission. From every point of view the expedition had been successful, and on the last day of the year the homeward journey was begun.

The Mozarts reached Salzburg on 5 January 1763—to depart again just five months later. Whatever the original motivation, Leopold's experience in Vienna had greatly sharpened his appetite: preparations for a westward tour to take in Paris and possibly London were set in progress at once. The only member of the family to be dismayed by the prospect was Anna Maria. She was no traveller, yet she knew her presence was essential to the well-being of the children. If anyone was the victim of these journeys, it was the mother, not the son. Wolfgang was ill again in January 1763, this time with rheumatic pains in the joints, but there is nothing to support the view that his early death was in some way abetted by the rigours of his childhood. When Mozart died in 1791, it was not from exhaustion or overwork—not directly, that is—but from uraemia, a kidney disease suspected by one physician as early as 1784. If our responses have not already been conditioned, he will appear to us in the later 1760s and 1770s as robust rather than sickly.

The westward expedition began on 9 June. Both the route and the timetable were flexible, as they needed to be; for it was summer, and so the people that mattered were not necessarily in predictable places. Leopold's skill and patience would have been the envy of any travelling impresario, and his critical appraisal of the high and mighty would at times have pleased even Voltaire. The scope of Wolfgang's performances had been enlarged to include the violin as well as the keyboard instruments. Much was made of the trick of covering the keyboard with a cloth, and the boy undertook to name any interval or chord played to him and to improvise 'in all keys, even the most difficult'. How far the emphasis was put on 'wizardry' depended on those present and the limits of their musicality. Had he been content merely to take the money of gullible sentimentalists, Leopold would not have been Leopold. He was anxious that the genuinely musical should appreciate his children's musicianship.

Despite some vivid glimpses of Wolfgang in action, the music that he played remains largely hidden. If the manuscript music-books compiled for him by Leopold are any indication, then dances by Telemann and short pieces by C. P. E. Bach and Hasse may well have been included. Much of the time, however, he played at sight what was put before him. In London, for instance, the king gave him pieces by Handel, Wagenseil and Abel, and in Paris he played music by two resident German musicians, Johann Schobert and Gottfried Eckhardt. The emphasis, it seems, was less on a prepared repertory than on brilliant versatility.

The way westward was naturally through Munich, Augsburg and Stuttgart, each of which seemed a promising centre. Despite, or because of, the earlier visit, there were notable successes at Munich, but Leopold's native Augsburg proved disappointing. There it was a matter of organizing public concerts, which was done with care but to little advantage. When it was found that the Württemberg court was not at Stuttgart but at the summer palace of Ludwigsburg, the route was modified accordingly. The Duke Karl Eugen, however, refused to hear the Mozart children, which Leopold at once attributed to intrigue: the court *Kapellmeister*, Niccolò Jommelli, was Italian, affluent and famous, and so was obviously responsible! Historical hindsight suggests that Leopold should have understood both men rather better. The Duke was notoriously autocratic and frequently at odds with his own subjects. Jommelli received the Mozarts warmly and heard Wolfgang play, but was thoughtless enough to express his amazement that 'a German child' should achieve such artistry.

Schwetzingen, the summer residence of the Duke Karl Theodor, Elector Palatine, brought very different fortunes. The famous Mannheim orchestra was there. 'It consists altogether of people who are young and of good character,' noted Leopold, 'not drunkards, gamblers

The Duke Karl Theodor, Elector Palatine from 1743. He was noted for his enthusiastic patronage of the arts and sciences, and at Mannheim his court orchestra, led by Johann Stamitz (1717–57), set new standards of brilliance and control. The Mannheim composers, encouraged to innovate, have an important place in the early history of the symphony.

Friedrich Melchior Grimm; engraving, after a portrait by Carmontelle, 1769. Grimm was a writer and publicist of the Enlightenment, an influential figure in Parisian cultural circles.

or dissolute fellows, so that both their behaviour and their playing are admirable.' The Duke kept the children busy for four hours and then paid handsomely. His *Kapellmeister*, Ignaz Holzbauer, had remained at Mannheim, where the Mozarts subsequently met him and became good friends. Leopold usually got on well with German musicians.

The journey continued through Worms to Mainz, which had a distinguished court and was a useful base for visits to a number of nearby towns. A concert at Frankfurt am Main was so successful that others had to be given. In one of the audiences was the 14-year-old Goethe, who was never to forget the impression made by the 'little man with his wig and sword'. Something of Leopold's methods emerges clearly now: always to stay at the best inn; to be seen with his children in the most likely places; to publish an extravagantly worded notice beforehand in the local newspaper, and to procure an introduction to some courtier or high official capable of turning the right locks. He knew that this last was most important, and the frequency with which he achieved it suggests that his human relations, as well as his planning, must have been excellent. At Coblenz, for instance, Count Pergen, with whom contact had been made at Frankfurt, 'took the children by the hand' and went directly to the Elector, who at once consented to hear them.

From Coblenz the route passed through Bonn, Cologne, Aix-la-Chapelle and Liège to Brussels. At Aix the Mozarts encountered Princess Amalia of Prussia, who was all rapture and no money. 'If the kisses which she gave my children, and to Wolfgang especially, had all been new *louis d'or*, we should be quite happy; but neither the innkeeper nor the postmaster are paid in kisses.' At Brussels, the capital of the Austrian Netherlands, Leopold was angered by Prince Charles of Lorraine, who kept the family waiting for a month: 'It looks as if nothing will come of it, for the Prince spends his time hunting, eating and drinking, and in the end it appears that he has no money'. This dismal verdict was to prove unfounded, for at long last a concert was given in the Prince's residence and was well paid for. One wonders whether recent successes had gone to Leopold's head a little, for he expected his children to be heard without delay, wherever he chose to present them, and he also expected a substantial profit. Undoubtedly his self-esteem had been heightened by the approbation of musicians, writers and others of his own class. In short, Leopold's, and very soon Wolfgang's, ambivalent attitude to princes and aristocrats may be seen as a microcosm of the developing social situation in the second half of the century.

In the middle of November 1763, the Mozarts entered Paris, where they remained for nearly five months. Even Leopold seems to have found the metropolitan atmosphere a little daunting at first, for neither

his experience nor his introductions counted for much. But Salzburg connections were soon utilized, and a little later the best of champions was found in the influential publicist and man of the Enlightenment, Melchior Grimm. Grimm managed everything, both at court and in Paris itself, and seems to have delighted in Leopold's gains. Christmas was spent at Versailles, where the family made a court appearance on New Year's Day. This entailed standing like lackeys behind the king and queen at a banquet, making conversation as required and humbly receiving the food that was proferred! Such was the mystique of Versailles, even under Louis XV, that Leopold thought they had been well done by. Nannerl noted that her brother 'played the organ in the court chapel, before the entire court, and won the applause of all'. Many invitations from the nobility followed, and two very successful concerts

The Palace of Versailles in the eighteenth century; oil painting by P. Martin, 1722. Versailles was the model for princely builders throughout Europe, not least the Duke Karl Theodor and Haydn's patron, Count Nikolaus Esterházy.

31

King George III and his family; oil painting by Johann Zoffany, 1770. The treatment of the King is highly stylized in the Baroque tradition and is in sharp contrast with the informal welcome enjoyed by the Mozarts in 1764.

were given in Paris. These last necessitated some special dispensation, for public music-making was limited by royal decree to the Opéra, the Théâtre Italien and the *Concert spirituel*.

Whatever doubts Leopold may have had about going on to England were overcome by the advice of his Parisian friends. London, they insisted, must on no account be missed, for its opportunities were unlimited. And so, on 22 April 1764, the Mozarts left their carriage at Calais and made the crossing to Dover. In London, they lodged at first off St Martin's Lane and later in Frith Street, Soho, and such was their reception that the visit became protracted until the summer of the following year. Here was a more open society and less condescension than they had previously experienced anywhere. But it is not at all clear how they spent their time, for the concerts and visiting performances do not seem to have been particularly numerous. We know that Leopold was ill with a throat infection for about three months, during which time Wolfgang applied himself to composition. We learn of three

32

appearances before George III and Queen Charlotte, both of whom were musical, of a charity concert in the Rotunda at Ranelagh in aid of a new maternity hospital—'a way to earn the love of this very remarkable nation', noted Leopold—and, indeed, of some concerts that were very profitable. We also learn of the Mozarts themselves seeing the sights: an aspect of their grand tour that is easily overlooked, but undoubtedly a real one, particularly in Brussels, Paris and London. Moreover, Wolfgang was enlarging his musical experience in a number of directions. The famous *castrato* (male soprano) Manzuoli volunteered to teach him the art of singing—prompted, it seems, by a regret that the boy's astonishing powers were at present purely instrumental. When the family returned to Paris, Grimm remarked on the expressiveness of Wolfgang's singing. Still more important, but almost equally hidden from us, is the time spent with two distinguished German musicians, Karl Friedrich Abel and Johann Christian Bach. Wolfgang enjoyed the close interest of Bach and in some sense became his composition pupil,

The Chinese House, the Rotunda and the Company in Masquerade in Ranelagh Gardens, 1759, by John Bowles. The Rotunda was a popular London concert hall. In letting Wolfgang play there at a charity concert on 29 June 1764, Leopold showed his business acumen.

33

but how formally it is hard to tell. Certainly Bach's highly polished and zestful Italianate style became second nature to the boy, so much so that some of the early compositions may easily be mistaken for Bach's music.

From a commercial viewpoint, the Mozarts may be said to have outstayed their welcome in London. The later concerts were less remunerative, and Leopold turned to a different clientele at the Swan and Hoop tavern, in the City, where the old trick of covering the keyboard with a cloth was revived. It was at this stage that the Hon. Daines Barrington, a Fellow of the Royal Society, made a quasi-scientific examination of Wolfgang, the report of which was published in the Society's *Philosophical Transactions*[4] and constitutes the most reliable account there is of the boy's musicianship. Among other tests, Barrington set before him some music in manuscript which he could not have seen before:

> The score was no sooner put upon his desk [that is, at the harpsichord], than he began to play the symphony in a most masterly manner, as well as in the time and stile which corresponded with the intention of the composer. . . .
>
> His astonishing readiness, however, did not arise merely from great practice; he had a thorough knowledge of the fundamental principles of composition, as, upon producing a treble, he immediately wrote a base under it, which, when tried, had a very good effect.
>
> He was also a great master of modulation, and his transitions from one key to another were excessively natural and judicious; he practised in this manner for a considerable time with an handkerchief over the keys of the harpsichord.
>
> The facts which I have been mentioning I was myself an eye witness of; to which I must add, that I have been informed by two or three able musicians, when Bach the celebrated composer had begun a fugue and left off abruptly, that little Mozart hath immediately taken it up, and worked it after a most masterly manner.

Shortly before leaving England, the Mozarts were persuaded by the Dutch ambassador to visit The Hague, which they did with a now familiar success. Despite increasing pressure from Archbishop Schrattenbach to return, their stay in Holland lasted seven months. This was partly because it was profitable and socially congenial, but also because of sickness. First Nannerl, then Wolfgang, went down with typhus and nearly died. The family remedies were the universal black powder and

Wolfgang in 'gala costume'. Like the matching portrait of Nannerl (see p. 27), this oil painting is probably by Pietro Antonio Lorenzoni, Salzburg, 1763.

34

Markgraf powder and special Masses in Salzburg churches—five for Nannerl, nine for Wolfgang. That the children survived is evidence of a remarkable stamina, and perhaps of the skill of the senior court physician, though even he seems to have despaired of their chances.

When the homeward journey was resumed, Brussels and Paris were revisited, after which a southerly route was taken: through Dijon and Lyons, then across Switzerland—there were notable stops at Geneva, Lausanne, Berne and Zurich—and eventually through Bavaria with a further visit to Munich. The original intention had been to visit northern Italy as well, but the pressure from Salzburg could no longer be ignored. When the family reached home on 30 November 1766, it was after an absence of nearly three and a half years: Nannerl was a self-assured young woman of fifteen, and Wolfgang was a seemingly unspoilt ten-year-old.

Unspoilt? It would scarcely have been surprising had he become insufferable. In fact, however, nobody seems to have found him so: at least, nobody whose comments have come down to us. Many, including Barrington, remarked on the ordinariness of his general behaviour. A part of the explanation may well lie in the close family discipline and in Leopold's insistence that there was always much to be learned. Important, too, is the seriousness of Wolfgang's commitment to what he was doing—a seriousness beyond self-conceit. Bumptiously exuberant he certainly was, but it is hard to detect affectation or a wilful flaunting of success.

The immediate effect of the grand tour was that of a musical education such as no other young musician, before or since, has ever received. The value in respect of performing skills needs no underlining. Less obvious, perhaps, is the impact on a child whose creative awareness was developing rapidly. Bearing in mind Wolfgang's hyper-receptiveness, it would be hard to exaggerate the formative effect of exposure to so wide a range of music and musicians. In terms of style alone, he learned more by direct experience than he could ever have done theoretically in Salzburg. The only significant school not obviously encountered, though it cannot be ruled out, was the north German, personified by C. P. E. Bach with whose work he already had some acquaintance. Otherwise, virtually every current style and genre was met with, responded to, discussed; often discussed with outstanding resident musicians, and always with Leopold, who seems never to have missed an educational opportunity.

No wonder we gain the impression that Wolfgang, as the tour developed, and especially in the western capitals, became more and more preoccupied with composition. In Paris, London and Amsterdam, harpsichord sonatas with violin accompaniment—at the time, the only form of 'violin sonata'—were written and published. In London, under the influence of J. C. Bach, he wrote his first symphonies (K. 16 and 19), and on the return visit to Paris his first setting of the *Kyrie* (K. 33). Noting Wolfgang's progress in composition, Grimm remarked in the *Correspondance littéraire*:[5] 'He has even written several Italian operas, and I do not abandon the hope that before he is twelve years old he will have had an opera performed in some Italian theatre.' Grimm went on to predict that, 'if these children remain on this earth, they will not stay in Salzburg. Before long the rulers of all Europe will be disputing for possession of them.'

Neither of these expectations was realized. Grimm overlooked two important points, the first of which Leopold was already aware of, and the second he was soon to have impressed upon him: namely, that with every month that passed, the wonderchildren would seem less wonderful; and that, while a prodigy at the keyboard might be smiled upon by all, a talented boy composer would encounter vested interests. Both these points were borne out by the further visit to Vienna made by the Mozart family between September 1767 and January 1769.

Almost certainly, Leopold looked for a greater triumph than before. His children were renowned throughout Europe, and in Vienna the Archduchess Maria Josepha was to be married to the King of Naples. But things went badly from the start; an outbreak of smallpox carried off the young archduchess and came near to despatching both Nannerl and Wolfgang. So there were no festivities to be exploited; and when the Mozarts were received at court, it was more as past acquaintances than as continuing novelties. The widowed Maria Theresa—Franz I had died in 1765—showed little interest in music, but her son, the Emperor Joseph II, thought it a good idea that Wolfgang should write an Italian opera for Vienna and conduct it himself from the harpsichord.

Such was the origin of *La finta semplice* (K. 51), for which a contract was signed with Affligio, the semi-independent manager of the court opera, the fee being 100 ducats. The composition was completed in July 1768, but a production was not forthcoming. For six months, Leopold, all righteous indignation, tried to overcome the machinations of Affligio, but without success. The further he went, the worse the situation became, until it seemed that everyone concerned, the singers included, had become hostile. Affligio was an adventurer and was at that time under financial pressure; on both counts he was a dangerous man and vulnerable to intrigues behind the scenes. What intrigues there were is not known, but it does seem likely that other composers, particularly those with operas in the production queue, were in some way involved.

After all, both Wolfgang's talent and Leopold's determination threatened their interests.

Leopold's stature, enhanced by his travels, emerges clearly from this episode. Not only did he marshal the support of such notables as Prince Kaunitz, the Duke of Braganza, the imperial court poet Pietro Metastasio, the future *Kapellmeister* Giuseppe Bonno and the very distinguished opera composer Johann Adolph Hasse, he also petitioned the emperor. Joseph, he tells us, 'was extremely gracious and promised full justice'; but nothing came of it—unless it was a certain coolness on the part of the Habsburgs ever after. From the Habsburgs' standpoint, the Mozarts were becoming troublemakers with ideas above their station: another social microcosm. Leopold, however, had already 'received from the Emperor himself all necessary recommendations to high personages in Florence, all the [Italian] lands in the Empire, and Naples'. Italy was the next objective.

The question of Leopold's motivation remains to be considered. By this time the advancement of his son's great gifts and the family's reputation—the two were inseparable—had become a way of life, and so the underlying motives are more than usually blurred. But the pursuit of professional and social esteem had from the outset been a powerful driving force, and this was undiminished. The importance of money-making is easily overstated. There were times, especially during the grand tour, when Leopold was much concerned with profit and loss; and rightly so, for the possible hazards were immense. It would be foolish to estimate the overall profit that was made, but it was certainly not enough to release the family from the archbishop's service. We do not know that such a possibility was every seriously entertained: perhaps the appropriate reference-point is Leopold's horror when in 1781 his son broke with Colloredo. From 1768 onwards, the advancement of Wolfgang as a composer was increasingly the concern to which everything else was secondary. Whenever Leopold himself formulated his motives, it was in terms of a duty to God 'to prove this miracle to the world'.

Tea at Prince de Conti's; oil painting by Michel-Barthélemy Ollivier, Paris, 1766. Wolfgang is at the harpsichord; the singer Pierre Jélyotte is tuning his guitar. Nearby, the prince has his back to the viewer.

MOZART'S EARLY COMPOSITIONS

The history of music shows plainly that Mozart grew up in an age of transition. The grandeur of Baroque music, be it J. S. Bach's, Handel's or Rameau's, had given way to Rococo elegance, but the achievement of the Classical style still lay in the future. Not that that achievement was an inevitable outcome, for the Rococo in music—the *style galant*, as it is commonly called—had many facets, some of them more courtly, others more popular or bourgeois. Hindsight distinguishes between the dissolution of Baroque ideals—in the music of Hasse, for instance—and the burgeoning of that new capability of conflict and development on which the rise of the symphony was to depend. The *galant* may therefore be said to have two faces, the one looking backward, the other forward. At the time, however, musicians were more concerned with stylistic fitness, relative to place and purpose, than with their own historical position. After all, the music of the 1750s and 1760s was usually written with some immediate object in view, and the role of those who wrote it was to no small extent that of superior artisans. The transition from artisan to artist, and the social tensions bound up with it, is one of the themes of Mozart's life.

Among the distinguishing features of *galant* music are an overriding concern with melodic and formal elegance and an avoidance of counterpoint. The melodic writing falls into fairly short 'sentences', punctuated by formal cadences, and the melody is supported by a light harmonic texture (homophony) with a slow rate of chord change. As the one melodic part is supreme, there is much scope for ornamentation, after the manner of a harpsichordist or of a coloratura soprano on the

Les Attributs de Musique, Jean-Baptiste Oudry (1686–1755). This still life, with its classical column and drinking song, shows the light-hearted elegance thought appropriate to music when Mozart was a young man.

41

operatic stage. Indeed, it was largely to Italian opera that the *galant* style owed its universality; for in the international courtly culture of the eighteenth century, Italian music was as paramount as French literature, and opera was everywhere the plaything of kings and princes. Only in France was there a separate operatic tradition, and that, too, had been founded by an Italian—Lully (originally Lulli).

Alongside the polished diversions of *galant* music, the contrapuntal skills of the Baroque tradition—canon and fugue, that is to say—were still a force to be reckoned with. These were thought of as 'learned' and old-fashioned, but were valued as mysteries of the craft of composition and were practised when occasion demanded. Fugal counterpoint remained indispensable in setting certain liturgical texts, which means that few serious composers could afford to neglect it. No wonder that so noted an authority in this field as Giovanni Battista Martini, known as 'Padre' Martini, with whom Wolfgang studied briefly at Bologna in 1770, enjoyed an international reputation. The most celebrated treatise on counterpoint was *Gradus ad Parnassum* (1725) by Johann Joseph Fux, *Kapellmeister* to Maria Theresa's father, the Emperor Charles VI. Several generations of composers were indebted to Fux, and we know that after the Mozarts' grand tour *Gradus ad Parnassum* formed part of Wolfgang's studies with his father.

Leopold Mozart believed in a mastery of all available techniques and directed Wolfgang's musical education to that end. We can recognize the ambitious, and frustrated, court musician in a number of his emphases: on observing the conventions, on imitating the best models, on not being excessively original—and, of course, on seeking to please. The attitudes inculcated in boyhood went very deep and did much to condition the 'presence' of the mature artist. Apart from his development of the piano concerto, which is the one big exception, Mozart was seldom an innovator in matters of form; time and again he created masterpieces with materials that were the merest commonplaces, and even at his most intense he usually preserved a gracious and considerate tone.

There are some striking points of contrast with the self-taught, untravelled Haydn, who, 'forced to become original',[6] proved to be the foremost innovator of his generation. Mozart's originality—individuality is perhaps the better word—expressed itself in all that we mean by the imaginative content of his music: new possibilities within the conventions; the ability to exceed even the ripest models, and at the same time to make simplicities memorable. . . . To name only one great work, *Le nozze di Figaro* (1786) exemplifies these assertions virtually throughout.

42

Giovanni Battista Martini, known as 'Padre' Martini (1706–84), priest, composer and pedagogue; *maestro di capella* to the Franciscan order at Bologna. His renown as a theorist and master of counterpoint brought musicians to Bologna from all over Europe.

Having outlined this perspective, we may more usefully consider some of the earliest of Mozart's compositions. It was during the later stages of the grand tour—from the first visit to Paris onwards—that the young boy's interest in composing became an undoubted involvement. His responsiveness to the music of Paris-based German musicians, notably Schobert, is evident in some of the violin sonatas, and the four piano concertos (K. 37 and 39–41) written in Salzburg in 1767 are adaptations of sonata movements by Schobert, Eckhardt, Raupach and others. Similarly, in London, Wolfgang had reworked sonatas by J. C. Bach. All that is remarkable is the age at which these things were done and the

capacity for assimilating, sifting and progressing. Such responsiveness is particularly striking in the first two symphonies (K. 16 and 19), written in London, for these reveal a progress from 'something childlike and halting' to 'the illusion of an adult composer'.[7] This is a matter, not of originality, but of a rapidly developing grasp of the techniques used by others in making *galant* symphonies.

The 'others' were J. C. Bach and Abel, whose concerts were an important feature of London musical life. Wolfgang copied out a symphony by Abel—an excellent way of discovering how it worked— but the Symphony in D (K. 19) shows clearly that Bach rather than Abel was his principal model. Indeed, Bach's influence was by no means temporary; though later supplanted by that of Haydn, it was the foremost means by which the young composer assimilated an up-to-date Italian style in both instrumental and vocal music.

Musically speaking, like Hasse before him, this youngest son of J. S. Bach had become completely Italianate. Unlike Hasse, whose work was pure Rococo, he was a master of the *galant* style in its dynamic, forward-looking aspects—hence his success with the London musical public— and was particularly noted for his 'singing allegros'—lively instrumental and orchestral movements in which the rhythmic and harmonic activity essential to the style is combined with an appealing lyricism. The first movements of many of his symphonies and piano concertos are clear examples. This achievement Mozart was to make his own—and, of course, to outstrip. Of the later Salzburg symphonies, No. 29 in A (K. 201) offers revealing evidence, and even in the finale of the *Jupiter* Symphony (K. 551)—the last of Mozart's symphonies, and the greatest finale—an extension of J. C. Bach's lyrical 'athleticism' is still fundamental.

At present, though, we are concerned with the pace at which a boy barely ten years old developed his grasp of compositional techniques. When the Mozarts returned from the grand tour, the archbishop was so incredulous of Leopold's claims that he had Wolfgang confined to a room in the Residenz to compose the first part of a Lenten oratorio. If Schrattenbach's intention was to bring his vice-*Kapellmeister* back to reality, then the move was ill-judged, for Wolfgang demonstrated a high degree of competence and his setting (K. 35) was duly performed, along with the second and third parts, composed respectively by Michael Haydn and Anton Adlgasser, the court organist. His models were his father's oratorios and those of Eberlin, an old-fashioned kind of music that he had not been concerned with of late, which again underlines his extraordinary receptiveness.

Much church music followed in the next few years: for the most part,

Johann Christian Bach (1735–82), as painted by Thomas Gainsborough in 1780. The youngest son of J. S. Bach, he trained in Italy and from 1762 was resident in London. His polished mastery of an up-to-date Italian style was a strong formative influence on Mozart from the age of eight.

settings of the mass, both festive and '*brevis*', for use at Salzburg. In general, these church compositions, especially the *Missae breves,* are typical of the culture to which they belong; they mix the *galant* and the 'learned', and their manner is operatic, frequently suggesting the gay Rococo church interiors of Austria and Bavaria. One of the earliest large-scale settings is the Mass in C (K. 66), known as the *Dominicus* Mass. Written in 1769 for the ordination of a son of Hagenauer, the Mozarts' landlord and friend, this reveals the boy composer at the top of his form. He also wrote the offertory, constructing it, as Einstein says, 'just like an Italian *sinfonia*: Allegro—Andante in F—Allegro'.[8] Still more remarkable is the Mass in C minor (K. 139), now widely accepted as the *Waisenhausmesse* (Orphanage Mass) written in Vienna for the festive dedication of the Orphanage Church on 7 December 1768. The patronage of Maria Theresa and the non-production of *La finta semplice*—see Chapter 2—made both Leopold and Wolfgang determined to use this opportunity to the full. Shortly afterwards, Leopold wrote to Hagenauer: 'The Mass . . . has restored that reputation which our enemies . . . intended to destroy, and, as the throng was amazing, has convinced the court and the public of the wickedness of our adversaries.'

Be that as it may, the *Waisenhausmesse* highlights the problems attaching to very early Mozart. Until the 1950s, when fresh evidence was adduced, scholars disputed the date of composition, for such grandeur and intensity—the *Crucifixus*, for instance—seemed almost unbelievable from one so young. Moreover, the manuscript score draws attention to Leopold's presence, for the continuo figuration—but no notation—is in his hand. To what extent was 'presence' active involvement? The perspective in which these problems should be viewed is provided by the fact that even the most arresting passages have their precedents in the music of Gluck, Hasse, Eberlin and others, including Leopold himself. But the level of creative emulation remains astonishing.

The first work for the theatre that catches our attention is not *La finta semplice* but the slightly earlier *Bastien und Bastienne* (K. 50), a *Singspiel* (German operetta) of French origin with music in the manner of the comic operas that Wolfgang had experienced in Paris. This simple pastoral diversion is exactly to scale and full of life, and we can still delight in it today; *La finta semplice*, however, like so many Italian comic operas of the time, is largely routine. The earliest Italian opera by Mozart worthy of note is *Mitridate, Rè di Ponto* (K. 87), a work in the 'serious' or tragic convention (*opera seria*). Written in 1770 for production at Milan, this is one of the fruits of the first visit to Italy begun when the composer was not quite fourteen.

For the next three years, Italy, and especially Milan, was at the centre of the Mozarts' ambitions. Of the three Italian journeys, only the first was an exhibition tour on the familiar pattern; the second and third were professional visits by a young composer under contract. These were years of rapid development, and even at the outset the travelling wonderchild seems appreciably older and more mature. This is partly because of his letters home—his mother and sister remained in Salzburg—but also there is much that suggests a different quality of response, especially among musicians. The public successes at Rovereto, Verona, Mantua and elsewhere have a familiar ring, the only difference being the greater excitability of the Italians who crowded the churches where Wolfgang was to play the organ. To established musicians, however, he was now less a 'phenomenon of nature', more a greatly gifted young colleague: an important shift in attitude, already foreshadowed during the *Finta semplice* affair in Vienna.

At Milan the Mozarts were received by Count Firmian, the governor-general of Lombardy and younger brother of a former archbishop of Salzburg. Needless to say, Leopold's exploitation of connections, however tenuous, was as masterly as ever, and in Milan he acquired letters of commendation to Parma, Bologna and Florence. Count Firmian proved a good friend, providing several opportunities, arranging for the commission of *Mitridate* and introducing Wolfgang to Sammartini. By then the 'grand old man' of north Italian music, Giovanni Battista Sammartini was the most influential figure among the first generation of Italian symphonists. Haydn dismissed him as a 'scribbler', but the young Mozart was impressed, which means that he found something worth assimilating and emulating: his first string quartet (K.80), written at an inn on the way to Parma, certainly reflects Sammartini's style.

At Bologna, 'Padre' Martini was visited twice. On each occasion Wolfgang wrote a fugue which was examined and highly commended. There was also a most successful concert under the enthusiastic patronage of Count Pallavicini: Wolfgang directed the orchestra and received a fee amounting to two-thirds of the sum paid to all the other musicians. Only the desire to be in Rome for Easter (1770) led Leopold to hurry on to Florence, where Wolfgang began a warm friendship with the younger Thomas Linley, a highly gifted English musician of his own age. On parting, both boys shed tears.

Rome was reached just in time for the performance in the Sistine Chapel during Holy Week of Allegri's *Miserere*, a nine-part choral work supposedly the exclusive property of the papal choir. According to Leopold, immediately after the service Wolfgang wrote out the work from memory, and the accuracy of his version was attested by a member

A view of Rome and the Tiber in the eighteenth century, by Gaspar van Wittel. The Mozarts, father and son, reached Rome in time for Easter 1770.

of the choir. Not surprisingly, much is made of this feat in the Mozart mythology. If it was what it appears to have been, then we have to conclude that few musicians of any age have demonstrated a comparable ear and faculty for retention. However, the *Miserere* is known to have been performed in Vienna, so copies of it, illicit or otherwise, must have existed. Had the Mozarts seen a copy? And, if so, was the feat carefully planned? It is not hard to imagine Leopold hastening to Rome 'with intent'—at the time he was repeatedly declaring that Wolfgang was 13 instead of 14. But even then, unless they had a copy with them, which seems unlikely, the achievement remains impressive.

Rome proved to be a big success socially, and so it should have done after 20 letters of recommendation. At the Vatican on Holy Thursday the Mozarts even gatecrashed the cardinals' table, Leopold ordering his servant 'to call out to the armoured Swiss guards to make way'. There was another nice touch on the eve of departure: because the road to Naples was notorious for bandits, Leopold contrived an escort of Augustinian monks! This also solved the problem of accommodation en route, for there were Augustinian monasteries at suitable distances.

Naples was the home of Italian opera, and to a large extent the arbiter of fashion. In a letter to Nannerl dated 5 June 1770, Wolfgang remarks on Jommelli's *Armida abbandonata*, which 'is beautiful, but too serious and old-fashioned'. Despite the composer's reputation in Germany, this

opera was a failure because it was out of step with the latest Neapolitan manner: a lesson not lost on either of the Mozarts, particularly with the commission for Milan already assured, to say nothing of the offers regretfully declined at Bologna, Rome and Naples itself. Among the other operas attended were works by Niccolò Piccinni and Giovanni Paisiello, two of the most polished exponents of the art, though subsequently quite eclipsed by Mozart's achievement. The musical importance of Naples during the middle decades of the century can hardly be exaggerated. Initially, the slimming away of counterpoint and the move towards a more athletic, homophonic style received its greatest impetus from Neapolitan 'taste'.

On the return journey northwards some notable honours were received. Pope Clement XIV conferred on Wolfgang the highest class of the Order of the Golden Spur, an honour accorded only one musician before him, the great Lassus, in the sixteenth century. The extraordinary nature of this event has seldom been remarked on. If for one moment we forget the magic name Mozart and note that 'knighthood' was conferred on a boy of 14 who had 'from earliest youth distinguished himself in the sweetest fashion in playing the harpsichord', then some explanation will be called for. But all we know is that the papal Secretary of State, who was actively involved in the award, had taken a liking to Wolfgang. What was Leopold's role? If the facts were fully known, this might

Naples, the royal palace, by the same painter as the view of Rome (opposite). 'The King', reported Mozart, 'has had a rough Neapolitan upbringing and in the opera he always stands on a stool so as to look a little taller than the Queen.'

49

prove to be perhaps his most accomplished diplomatic coup.

Of much greater musical significance is Wolfgang's election to membership of the renowned *Accademia filarmonica* of Bologna. Although 20 was the statutory minimum age, on examination he was elected unanimously. His 'exercise'—written, Leopold tells us, 'in a good half-hour'—was the antiphon, *Quaerite primum regnum Dei* (K. 86). This and the *Miserere* with organ continuo (K. 85) reflect the boy's renewed acquaintance with Martini, who seems to have been the first to awaken his interest in choral polyphony. Early in the following year, after the highly successful production of *Mitridate* at the Ducal Theatre, Milan, the *Accademia filarmonica* of Verona likewise elected Wolfgang a member.

The composition and preparation of *Mitridate* dominated the autumn and early winter. Such a commission was executed to suit the voices of particular singers, so work on the arias and ensembles could not go far until the cast was known. The recitatives were begun at Bologna, but all the more serious composing awaited the return to Milan on 18 October. As late as 24 November, Leopold reported that Wolfgang had written only one aria for the *primo uomo*—the *castrato*, Benedetti—who did not reach Milan until 1 December. There were the usual problems with the cast, though in a fairly mild form: eighteenth-century opera singers, if good enough, could almost literally 'call the tune'; they demanded more arias, or more imposing arias, and resorted to tantrums to get their way. The first performance, directed by Wolfgang from the harpsichord, took place on 26 December and was so successful that a run of 20 performances ensued and a second opera, to be produced during the carnival of 1773, was commissioned.

That a German boy composer should have achieved such a triumph in one of the principal Italian centres is quite extraordinary. The nineteenth-century Mozart scholar, Friedrich Chrysander, provides the basis for an explanation: 'With great studiousness and completely absorbed in his task, Mozart studied those works of the Italian theatre which were the most highly valued at the time, and impressed their art and effects on his mind'.[9] Indeed, the first modern revival, at Salzburg in 1971, showed how well the composer had heeded everything the conventions required; but, surprisingly, one also glimpsed intimations of a great tragic artist in the making, and even something of the humanity of *Figaro*. However, such hindsight can be fanciful, and there is no doubt that most of *Mitridate* is skilful imitation.

The second visit to Italy, begun in August 1771, was occasioned by yet another commission from Milan. This was for the serenata, *Ascanio in Alba* (K. 111), to be performed in October after the wedding of the Archduke Ferdinand, Governor of Lombardy, and the Princess Beatrice

Mozart as a Knight of the Golden Spur; oil painting by an unknown artist (Salzburg, 1777). This is a copy made for 'Padre' Martini; the original is lost.

50

The wedding of the Archduke
Ferdinand and the Princess Maria
Beatrice d'Este in Milan
Cathedral, 16 October 1771;
engraving by Pietro Antonio
Novelli after a painting by
Antonio Zatti. Mozart's
contribution to the festivities was
a serenata, *Ascanio in Alba*, which
was well liked.

of Modena. Due mainly to bureaucratic muddle and delay—the
commission was an imperial one, nominally Maria Theresa's—
Wolfgang had little time for the completion of this two-act dramatic
work, some of which was written under conditions that many
composers would consider intolerable. Thus Wolfgang to his sister on 24
August:

> Upstairs we have a violinist, downstairs another one, in the
> next room a singing-master who gives lessons, and in the other
> room opposite ours an oboist. That is good fun when you are
> composing! It gives you plenty of ideas.

Ascanio in Alba was very successful; according to Leopold, it
'overwhelmed Hasse's opera' (*Ruggiero*) given the day before, and Hasse

himself is said to have remarked, 'This boy will consign us all to oblivion.' No wonder Leopold decided to remain in Milan, hoping that when the archduke returned from his honeymoon there would be a permanent appointment for Wolfgang. Such hopes, it seems, were not unfounded, but Maria Theresa wrote to her son instructing him not to 'burden himself with a composer or similar useless people who run about the world like beggars'. That thought-provoking letter was written in December, and the archduke did as he was told. The Mozarts left at once and were back in Salzburg a week before Christmas. The old empress had struck a very jarring note.

The third Italian journey, again to Milan, was for the composition and production of *Lucio Silla* (K. 135), the *opera seria* commissioned on the strength of *Mitridate*. The late arrival of some of the singers, notably the *prima donna*, Maria Anna de Amicis, and a very late substitute for the tenor, who was ill, demanded of Wolfgang not only rapidity but adaptability. He seems to have revelled in the challenge and to have satisfied even the difficult Amicis. The première was on 26 December 1772, and there were 25 subsequent performances. The response may well have been less demonstrative than when *Mitridate* was given—the composer was now almost 17—but it was hardly less positive. *Lucio Silla* was an undoubted success, more so, perhaps, than it deserved to be. The libretto is cold and formal, the music 'unequal in style, with no conception of dramatic unity', and many of the arias are 'probably more difficult than effective'.[10] Considered as a whole, it is less satisfactory than *Mitridate*, but two scenes for the heroine, Giunia, have a tragic power beyond anything in the earlier work. Where the text is worthy of an imaginative response, Wolfgang responded; elsewhere he provided what the conventions, and his singers, required.

These months and years in Italy brought a greatly deepened involvement in composition. The keyboard virtuoso receded; more striking still, a specifically Mozartian quality of expression began to emerge, even where imitation remained the basis. One work has a place in the permanent repertory: the well-known motet for soprano and orchestra, *Exsultate, jubilate* (K. 165), written for the *castrato* who had taken the principal role in *Lucio Silla*. Unless we include *Bastien und Bastienne*, this is the earliest Mozart classic.

Despite his preoccupation with operas and other vocal music, Wolfgang wrote a lot of orchestral works—symphonies, *divertimenti* and the like—and a number of string quartets. The latter, though not now considered important, show rapid progress from *divertimento* music in four parts to a genuine chamber-musical style. The six quartets K. 155–60 are Italianate—they were written on the way to Milan at the end of October 1772, or in Milan itself—but contain many pointers to the mature Viennese quartets; there are ideas for which no precedent has been found, and passages that only Mozart could have created.

It is in his symphonies that the young composer's development is clearest and most accessible to listeners today. All these have been recorded. Because there were fewer constraints than in *opera seria* or in church music, the symphonies reveal a diversity of models and approaches, and this in turn underlines the power of creative emulation. Perhaps the first symphony that should really be noted is No. 8 in D (K. 48), written in Vienna in 1768. For this is a fully-fledged Viennese symphony, different in style from the works that preceded it, and yet wonderfully firm and assured: the finale is like good Dittersdorf, who was no mean composer. No. 10 in G (K. 74), written in Milan at the end of 1770, is Italianate again with the zestful spirit of *opera buffa* in its outer movements. Balance, proportion, fine detail and a polished finish: these qualities are at once impressive. More remarkable, however, is the strong follow-through; only in the very earliest symphonies is there anything of the short-windedness—a stop-and-start-again effect—typical of the *galant* style. During the years 1770 to 1772, Wolfgang wrote no fewer than twenty symphonies, and in 1773 another seven. Not until the summer of 1788 was he again to give the form such concentrated attention. Nearly all these works make some new exploration, and many reflect the musical environment in which they were created. For example, No. 20 in D (K. 133), one of three written in Salzburg in the summer of 1772 between the second and third visits to Italy, combines Austrian and Italian qualities in a way that insists on the epithet Mozartian. The richness and breadth of the opening movement would alone make this symphony of special interest; but there is also a substantial minuet, a finale that is not simply *buffo*, and a slow movement in which a new gloss is given to a familiar type of serenade music. This last sounds Haydnesque, though the model may well have been Michael Haydn rather than Joseph. In Salzburg, serenades and *divertimenti* figured as prominently as church music in Wolfgang's production.

When the Mozarts left Italy for the third, and last, time, it can only have been with regret and misgiving as well as satisfaction. Much success had been theirs, but once again they had lingered on to no avail in expectation of an appointment for Wolfgang. And they knew that in Salzburg a new dispensation, very different from the old, was beginning to make itself felt.

A NEW ORDER IN SALZBURG

Archbishop Schrattenbach had died in December 1771, and had been succeeded by Hieronymus Joseph von Paula, Count of Colloredo, formerly the prince-bishop of Gurk. For the celebrations following the formal installation of Colloredo in April 1772, Wolfgang had written *Il sogno di Scipione* (K. 126), a *festa teatrale* in one act. At first, the Mozarts had reason to look favourably upon the new archbishop, for he required more music and seemed disposed to reward good work. In August, Wolfgang was appointed *Konzertmeister* (leader of the orchestra) with a salary of 150 gulden, and a little later both father and son were given leave to make their third Italian journey. But the citizens of Salzburg did not warm to Colloredo, who was markedly different from his easy-going, if occasionally censorious, predecessor.

This difference was not simply a matter of personality and temperament; two generations were involved, and two conceptions of autocracy. Schrattenbach belonged to the late Baroque and was guided by tradition; but Colloredo, whose study was adorned with portraits of Rousseau and Voltaire, was essentially a ruler of the new age. Arthur Hutchings sums him up succinctly: 'He was neither voluptuary nor obscurantist, but very much a product of the Enlightenment, determined to govern punctiliously and exact punctilious service, for he thought it his duty to educate.'[11] Here was a man of the same stamp as the 'enlightened' Emperor Joseph II—significantly, the imperial court had intervened to ensure his election—and his path of reform proved similarly thorny. He sought to rationalize the state administration, combat superstition and abolish customs that made for lethargy and

Hieronymus Joseph von Paula, Count of Colloredo, Prince-Archbishop of Salzburg from 1772; oil painting by Franz Xaver König, 1772. A minor exponent of 'enlightened despotism', he demanded good order and good service. The Mozarts' aspirations and independence offended on both counts.

disorder—excessive 'holy days', for instance. At the same time, he wished to put Salzburg on the cultural map, in which respect he must surely have accounted the Mozarts major assets. He was not unintelligent, though probably both insensitive and obstinate; if he recognized Wolfgang's artistic stature, he showed little capacity for accommodating it. Naturally, as a man of order, he found repeated absenteeism unacceptable. Faced with the Mozarts' determination to go their own way, he reacted boorishly.

Shortly after returning from Italy in March 1773, Leopold and his family moved from the Getreidegasse to a larger house in what was then the Hannibalplatz and is now the Makartplatz. This is across the river from the old town and near the entrance to the Mirabell Gardens. Known as the Dancing Master's House—or as Mozart's *Wohnhaus* (dwelling house)—this seventeenth-century residence had the attraction of eight fine rooms, light and spacious, one of them being a small concert-room. It was there that nearly all Wolfgang's subsequent Salzburg works were written. The move was prompted partly by the Italian experience—sunshine and heightened self-esteem—but also by practical considerations. As early as February 1771, Leopold had written from Venice to his wife: 'It has just struck me that we cannot go on living in our present home. Will you see whether we could not move somewhere else. We cannot continue to sleep like soldiers. Wolfgang is no longer seven years old . . . .'

Leopold's failure to procure a worthy appointment for his son in Milan or Florence had left him eager for fresh opportunities. One soon presented itself, the archbishop having decided to make an extended visit to Vienna during the summer months. The Mozarts sought, and were granted, leave of absence and likewise travelled to Vienna, where they remained from the middle of July until the end of September. It is clear that they went the social round and were politely received by Maria Theresa—she was 'very gracious', Leopold says—but there is nothing that suggests any prospect of employment. Why was the visit so prolonged despite financial strain? Was it in the hope of approaching Joseph II when he returned from Poland in September? If so, nothing came of it. This episode remains a mystery. In his letters to his wife, Leopold was unusually guarded, which suggests that he was playing for high stakes. Gossips in Salzburg said that the sickness of the imperial *Kapellmeister*, Florian Leopold Gassmann—he died in the following January—was what the visit was about! Mozart scholars have generally dismissed this notion. Leopold, they say, was too level-headed to suppose that a 17-year-old, however gifted, would be appointed to such a post. Nonetheless, a more likely explanation has yet to be provided.

The Mozart family, by Johann Nepomuk della Croce, Salzburg, 1780–81. The portrait of Anna Maria, who had died in Paris in 1778, is based on that attributed to Lorenzoni (see p. 17). It says much for the seriousness of della Croce's painting that, in 1819, Nannerl recommended it as a model for the posthumous portrait of her brother by Barbara Krafft (see p. 151).

Mozarts Wohnhaus (dwelling-house), also known as the Dancing Master's House; lithograph after G. Pezold, *c.* 1840. The Mozart family moved from the Löchelplatz (Getreidegasse) in 1773, and Leopold lived here until his death in 1787. This drawing shows the spaciousness of the Hannibalplatz (Makartplatz) and in the background the monastery on the Kapuzinerberg.

Meanwhile, Wolfgang was writing music, including a set of six string quartets (K. 168–73). It has been suggested that these quartets were prompted by Leopold; if so, it is probable that he intended them for the eyes of the quartet-playing emperor. For us, however, the special interest is once again the spirit of creative emulation. Wolfgang had been studying Haydn's newly published string quartets Opps. 17 and 20, and this is shown throughout the set: in, for example, the first-movement variations of K. 170, the slow introduction to K. 171, the serenade-like slow movements, the two finales in fugal style. . . . These are Viennese quartets, very different from the ones written in Milan, and their best movements reveal a deeper quality of expression than any of the previous instrumental works. The finest is undoubtedly the last, in D minor (K. 173), the only weakness being the fugal finale, which is studious rather than felt and stylistically unconvincing. This is not surprising, for the fugal finales in Haydn's Op. 20 are also somewhat awkward, suggesting that Baroque techniques have been bent to the

60

composer's purpose rather than effectively transformed. As Einstein puts it, 'Mozart was, so to say, confused by Haydn', and 'Haydn himself was a bit confused'.

Haydn's Op. 20—the so-called *Sun* Quartets (1772)—was a major achievement breaking new ground. Like the minor-key symphonies written at about the same time—especially Nos. 39, 44 and 49—Op. 20 represents Haydn's dissatisfaction with a shallow, courtly art and his desire to produce something more genuinely expressive and keenly felt. This development has been associated, somewhat over-simply, with the *Sturm und Drang* (Storm and Stress) movement in German literature, of which Goethe's *The Sorrows of Young Werther* (1774) is the most celebrated example. Certainly both these phenomena were reactions to the social and cultural *status quo*. In music, the rejection of *galant* platitudes was not confined to Haydn; most of the established Viennese composers started writing strenuously in minor keys. Gassmann, for instance, wrote six quartets with every other movement in fugal style. As well as some three or four quartet movements—the C minor *Andante* from K. 171 is notable because it is individual and fully realized—this new spirit drew from Wolfgang a Symphony in G minor (K. 183, not to be confused with K. 550) that has long been labelled *Sturm und Drang*. The over-zealous have sought some personal explanation for this isolated work—adolescence, discontent with Salzburg, disappointment in love—but it seems more likely that the composer was seeing what he could do in this impassioned style. Assured and convincing though it is, K. 183 should ultimately be seen as a stylistic exercise.

Another isolated work, written in Salzburg in the spring of 1773 and revised in December, is Wolfgang's first string quintet, in B flat (K. 174). It was Michael Haydn who established the quintet with two violas, and works of his would seem to have prompted both versions of K. 174. This is an accomplished piece of writing, for the most part true chamber music, and often unmistakably Mozartian. The finale is a large-scale sonata form, in structural grasp and range of expression the most distinguished so far; there is even a nicely proportioned *fausse reprise* (false recapitulation), a device seldom found in Mozart. (The dramatic effect is keenly judged: six bars of apparently innocent recapitulation lead to a chord that destroys at a blow the sense of home-coming; the process is repeated a tone higher, in the minor, and the theme's characteristic note-pattern is then subjected to a piece of development far removed from its original spirit.) In these later Salzburg years, Michael Haydn was an important influence; he was closely associated with the reformed church music decreed by Colloredo, but was also an experienced composer of *divertimenti*, symphonies and chamber music, capable of retaining the admiration and respect of the mature Mozart. When in 1791 the latter was planning his Requiem (K. 626), it was to Michael Haydn's Requiem for Schrattenbach that he turned for a model.

The years from 1774 to 1777 were productive of a great deal of music—and of a growing discontent with the scope that Salzburg offered. How far this discontent was fostered by Leopold is difficult to assess. Without a doubt, Wolfgang had it impressed upon him that, operatically at least, fulfilment could only be achieved elsewhere, and that he should be satisfied with nothing less than a senior appointment at one of the noted musical centres. But the habit of years—more than ten years, in fact—was surely as strong a factor: the seasoned traveller with so much to offer found it hard to stay at home. Still, in addition to church music, and minuets, marches and *divertimenti* for the court, these years brought forth a number of works of classic status, among them the Bassoon Concerto (K. 191), the Symphony No. 29 in A (K. 201), the five Violin Concertos (K. 207, 211, 216, 218 and 219), the *Serenata notturna* (K. 239), the *Haffner* Serenade (K. 250) and the Piano Concerto in E flat (K. 271).

Some of these works combine a youthful gaiety and ease with the utmost refinement, composure and perfection of form; they are completely mature expressions of the 20-year-old musician. Listening to the Symphony No. 29, in which the feline in Mozart emerges as never before, or to the exquisite *Serenata notturna* for string quartet, string orchestra and timpani, or to any of the last three violin concertos, one is aware of human and musical qualities that are fundamental to Mozart's peculiar appeal. These are the qualities that were to immortalize the role of Cherubino (*Figaro*), a young man in love with love, to render magical the fairy-tale element in *Die Zauberflöte* (The Magic Flute), to transmute suffering into something that sings and dances—the String Quintet in G minor (K. 516) or the last piano concerto (K. 595)—and to give simple expressions in major keys a heart-rending pathos. In our efforts to describe such qualities, we tend to use words like 'love', 'beauty' and 'purity', giving them a wider-eyed connotation than we might otherwise allow. But essentially, at the point where the music begins, words become clumsy and inept.

The theatrical works from these years are *La finta giardiniera* (The Pretended Garden-Girl, K. 196) and *Il Rè pastore* (The Shepherd King, K. 208), the one an *opera buffa* commissioned by Munich, the other a *festa teatrale* required by the archbishop for the entertainment of the Archduke Maximilian. The Munich commission was particularly important and both Wolfgang and his father saw it as a stepping-stone to preferment. Moreover, since the Elector of Bavaria had personally

La finta giardiniera—or rather, a version of it with a German text; title page of vocal score, Mannheim, 1829(?). During much of the nineteenth century it was mainly in such versions, with spoken dialogue, that Mozart's Italian operas gained the attention of German audiences.

62

DIE
GAERTNERIN AUS LIEBE
OPER IN DREI AUFZÜGEN

VON

W. A. MOZART

In vollständigem Clavierauszug mit deutschem Texte, und zugleich für das
Piano Forte allein

IHRER

Königlichen Hoheit der Frau Markgräfin

LEOPOLD zu BADEN

in tiefster Ehrfurcht zugeeignet von dem
Verleger

Wohlfeile Ausgabe von W. A. Mozart's sämmtlichen Opern 6te Lieferung

MANNHEIM
bei Carl Ferdinand Heckel

Subscriptions Preis fl. 4.   Laden Preis fl. 6.

requested that the composer be present, the archbishop could hardly obstruct. Leopold would have us believe that permission was granted grudgingly; nonetheless, he too was able to be present. In a letter to his mother, Wolfgang reported on the first performance with great enthusiasm; and the poet Schubart wrote: 'If Mozart is not a forced hothouse plant, he will certainly become one of the greatest composers of music who ever lived.'[12] But *La finta giardiniera* was not taken up, whereas the opera by Pasquale Anfossi on the same libretto, composed only a few months before, was highly successful both in Italy and in Germany. There is no doubt as to which was the richer score—Anfossi was a slick, superficial composer who did what was expected—and the charge of 'over-richness', if only implicit on this occasion, was to be heard many times later on. To us, the mature Mozart's precision is a form of perfection; but his contemporaries found extravagance, 'too many notes', 'more genius than taste' . . . . Significantly, Schubart thought of Mozart as a *Sturm und Drang* artist.

During 1776 the situation in Salzburg deteriorated. Colloredo was making economies; bent on retrenchment and reform, he closed the small court theatre, and his requirements of the *Kapelle* were becoming more exacting, largely in the spirit of value for money. At about the same time he seems to have taken a personal dislike to the Mozarts. It is not hard to imagine that there were many ways in which both Leopold and Wolfgang assumed a special status within the *Kapelle*. From Colloredo's standpoint, they were too independent and therefore subversive of good discipline. In a letter to 'Padre' Martini, Leopold reported that the archbishop had asserted that Wolfgang 'knows nothing' and 'ought to go to a conservatory in Naples in order to learn music'. Whether this withering snub was on impulse or an act of policy remains unclear; but the effect on Leopold was profound, for in one sentence his dearest life's work had been discounted completely and thrown in his face. Months later, when Wolfgang was at Mannheim, Leopold wrote most feelingly of this episode, declaring that it had preyed on his mind and kept him from sleeping.

Wolfgang, too, had written to Martini:

> Alas, that we are so far apart, my dear Signor Padre Maestro! If we were together, I should have so many things to tell you. . . . I never cease to grieve that I am far away from that one person in the world whom I love, revere and esteem most of all. . . .

Clearly, he was seeking an invitation to Bologna, which must have seemed an excellent base for work throughout Italy, the land where success had been not only sweet but almost invariable. Meanwhile, Leopold was preparing a new assault on the musical centres of western Europe, and this was the project that came to fruition, though not in the way originally intended.

When father and son sought leave of absence in March 1777, the archbishop had good grounds for his refusal: an impending visit by the emperor. Later, however, he expressed his feelings on the matter in terms strikingly reminiscent of Maria Theresa; he did not wish his servants to go 'running around like beggars'. For himself, Leopold accepted the inevitable, but he thought that the tour might go forward with Anna Maria taking his place. Accordingly, in August, Wolfgang petitioned the archbishop for his dismissal. The letter is both flowery and artful, citing biblical precept and the archbishop's former words; even when apparently obsequious, it contrives to be critical: surely the hand of Leopold is present here. Colloredo's response was prompt and unequivocal: '. . . father and son, in accordance with the Gospel, have permission to seek their fortune elsewhere'. In other words, both were sacked! Leopold succeeded in retaining his post, but his self-esteem was badly tarnished. The subsequent departure of his wife and son moved him deeply:

> After you both had left, I walked up our steps very wearily and threw myself down on a chair. When we said good-bye, I made great efforts to restrain myself in order not to make our parting too painful; and in the rush and flurry I forgot to give my son a father's blessing.

His spirit curbed, if not somewhat broken, Leopold seems suddenly to have grown older, almost visibly. Wolfgang, however, urged his father to 'laugh heartily and be jolly and cheerful and always remember, as we do, that Mufti H. C. [the archbishop] is a prick, but that God is compassionate . . . .' Here, in a sentence, is one of Mozart's basic responses to life; it is a part, not the whole of his 'C major' view of things, a carefree optimism that Leopold considered irresponsible. In practical human terms, Leopold was right, and it caused him much anxiety. This can be seen in the correspondence in the ensuing 12 months. Wolfgang, now 21, began by writing as boyishly as when he was in Italy, but Leopold's mixture of reproaches, exhortations and sound advice obliged him to adopt a more diplomatic tone. Throughout the tour, what most worried Leopold was his son's 'familiar fault': basically, soft-heartedness, lack of purpose, a readiness to be 'led away by sudden ideas and illusory visions'.

65

Maria Anna Thekla Mozart, the 'little cousin' of Augsburg, 'beautiful, intelligent, charming, clever and gay'; pencil drawing, 1777/8.

Moreover, he had little confidence that Anna Maria would be an effective goad, for mother and son were too much alike.

Although exaggerated and, at times, even slightly hysterical, Leopold's analysis was not unsound. As Wolfgang and his mother went on from Munich to Augsburg, to Mannheim, and eventually to Paris, there were indeed 'illusory visions'; none of the prospects discussed in letters home had any real substance. But if deception was involved, it was mostly self-deception. In Paris the shrewd, observant Grimm confirmed Leopold's misgivings: 'Wolfgang is too generous, not pushing, too easily taken in, too little concerned with the means that lead to fortune'. Curiously, when nothing was at stake, Wolfgang could be brilliantly perceptive. His comments on other musicians were often cruelly penetrating. In that, as in his self-esteem, he was like his father.

The tour brought much of interest, both musically and socially, but also many irksome calls at the behest of Leopold. So far as a possible appointment was concerned, the experience at Munich may be regarded as typical. Wolfgang's account of his audience with the Elector Maximilian Joseph leaves one wondering what impression he made:

> When the Elector came up to me, I said: 'Your Highness will allow me to throw myself most humbly at your feet and offer you my services.' 'So you have left Salzburg for good?' 'Yes, your Highness, for good.' 'How is that? Have you had a row with him?' 'Not at all, your Highness. I only asked him for permission to travel, which he refused. So I was compelled to take this step, though indeed I had long been intending to clear out. For Salzburg is no place for me, I can assure you.' 'Good heavens! There's a young man for you! But your father is still in Salzburg?' 'Yes, your Highness. He too throws himself most humbly at your feet. . . . My sole wish is to serve your Highness, who himself is such a great—' 'Yes, my dear boy, but I have no vacancy. I am sorry. If only there were a vacancy—' 'I assure your Highness that I should not fail to do credit to Munich.' 'I know. But it is no good, for there is no vacancy here.' This he said as he walked away. . . .

How clumsy Grimm would have considered such an approach! And in anyone else the mixture of cocksureness and pretended servility would have been mocked by Wolfgang himself.

At Augsburg there was much enjoyable but unremunerative music-making, and some diversion with the *Bäsle* (little cousin), Maria Anna Thekla Mozart. To Wolfgang, this outgoing, coltish child was

66

'beautiful, intelligent, charming, clever and gay. . . . Indeed, we two get on extremely well, for, like myself, she is a bit of a scamp. We both laugh at everyone and have great fun . . .'. What sort of fun? The uproarious, smutty letters that Wolfgang wrote to her afterwards have drawn much comment. 'Such childish obscenities, such ill-smelling bouquets,' comments Einstein, though he concedes that the writer found 'genuine amusement' in them. Probably the relationship was a little less 'innocent' than sentimentalists like to think, but doubtless it was characterized by playful high spirits rather than anything more erotic. While Wolfgang was at Mannheim, the *Bäsle* and he exchanged portraits, and this, too, was done in a scampish way.

The view that the adult Mozart was a practised libertine is a product of the darker type of Romantic imagination and has long been discredited. His relationships with women were unremarkable, and his marriage was both stable and happy. Once again, when the man is considered apart from the musician, it is his ordinariness that comes to the fore. But it is a highly impressionable ordinariness, a nature warm and generous and quick to respond to similar qualities in others. This capacity for easy

Munich in the eighteenth century, showing the old town hall and the vegetable market; coloured engraving by Georg Balthasar Probst. Both *La finta giardiniera* and *Idomeneo* (see Chapter 5) were written for the Bavarian court at Munich, where Mozart, in the later 1770s, was hopeful of finding an appointment.

Aloysia Lange, *née* Weber, as Zémire in Grétry's opera *Zémire et Azor*; engraving by Johannes Esaias Nilson, 1784. At Mannheim in 1777, Mozart was so infatuated with Aloysia that, despite her inexperience, he thought he could launch her as a *prima donna* in Italy.

friendship—in Schubert's generation, in Vienna, it would have made for bohemianism—largely determined the course of events during the winter spent at Mannheim. Three families in particular experienced, and in their different ways exploited, Wolfgang's friendship: those of the court *Konzertmeister*, Christian Cannabich, the flautist Johann Wendling and the copyist, prompter and minor singer Fridolin Weber.

Wendling and the oboist Ramm were seen by Anna Maria as corrupting influences with greater sway over her son than she herself enjoyed. Weber had four daughters, of whom the two eldest were talented singers. Wolfgang was at once attracted to Aloysia, the second daughter, and very soon he was in love with her. If his mother knew as much—how could she not have done?—she said nothing of it in her letters to Leopold. However, when Wolfgang became involved in an ill-conceived plan to travel with the Webers to Italy, where both Aloysia and himself would supposedly make their fortunes, Anna Maria expressed dismay and anxiety. She did so in a postscript to a letter in which Wolfgang had presented the plan in the best possible light:

> From this letter you will see that when Wolfgang makes new acquaintances, he immediately wants to sacrifice everything for them.
>
> It is true that she sings magnificently. But we must never neglect our own interests. I never felt comfortable about his association with Wendling and Ramm, but he never allowed me to make any objections and never listened to me.
>
> But as soon as he became acquainted with the Webers, he changed his mind immediately. In short, he prefers being with other people to being with me. I take exception to various things he does, and he does not like that. You must therefore consider what is to be done. . . .

Leopold was beside himself, for this exceeded his worst imaginings. He took two days (11 and 12 February 1778) writing his reply, which is surely the finest of his letters. In it, anger is tempered with regret, and worldly wisdom is reinforced by an appeal to filial and religious obligation. Having reminded Wolfgang of the purposes for which the journey was undertaken, he continues:

> . . . it now depends on you alone to raise yourself gradually to a position of eminence such as no musician has ever obtained. You owe that to the extraordinary talents which you have received from a beneficent God; and now it depends solely on

HOTEL OF THE III. MOORS AT AUGSBURGH.

HÔTEL AUX III. MAURES À AUGSBOURG.

ALBERGO DEI III. MORI IN AUGUSTA.

ges. u. gest. v. F. J. Edelwirth.

bey. A. Klauber in Augsburg.

J. G. Deuringers GASTHOF zu den Drey Mohren

in der

Maximilians Strasse in Augsburg.

your good sense and your way of life whether you die as an ordinary musician, utterly forgotten by the world, or as a famous *Kapellmeister*, of whom posterity will read—whether, captured by some soman, you die bedded on straw in an attic full of starving children, or whether, after a Christian life spent in contentment, honour and renown, you leave this world with your family well provided for and your name respected by all.

There follows a hard-hitting account of the failures, follies and mistakes at each stage of the journey, and then come the marching orders: '*Off with you to Paris!* and that soon! Find your place among great people. *Aut Caesar aut nihil.*'

The Three Moors Inn, Maximilianstrasse, Augsburg; engraving by E. P. Edelwirth. The Mozart family first stayed here during their 1763 tour, and then again in 1766.

69

Anna Maria had intended returning to Salzburg from Mannheim, but it was now thought politic that she should accompany Wolfgang to Paris. The journey took nine wearisome days, Paris being reached on 23 March. The scene was set for the culminating disaster, and this is underlined for us by the fact that even Leopold had a rose-tinted view of Parisian prospects. 'There', he writes, 'the nobility treat men of genius with the greatest deference, respect and courtesy.' Perhaps, but such civility did not necessarily mean genuine interest, let alone a willingness to pay. Leopold had immense confidence in Grimm with his network of social connections, and he urged Wolfgang to keep away from the well-known composers, especially Gluck, Piccinni and Grétry, whose malice he considered directly proportionate to their eminence. There was a brief encounter with Piccinni, who was 'perfectly polite'—naturally!—and Wolfgang also met the foremost Paris symphonist, François-Joseph Gossec, whom he described as 'my very good friend, and a very dry man'; otherwise, musical notabilities do not figure in his letters.

Grimm did what he could and even helped financially, but from the start things did not go well. Interest was shallow, and the only way of ensuring an income was by taking pupils. The Duc de Guines invited Wolfgang to teach composition to his daughter, an accomplished harpist, but as a pupil she proved 'heartily stupid and heartily lazy' and the agreed salary was whittled down. That was not unrepresentative of Wolfgang's experience. Moreover, it soon became clear that opportunities for composition would have to be fought for; the name Mozart had few of the advantages enjoyed in Italy or even in Germany. No wonder that Paris quickly turned sour. For one thing, Wolfgang's heart was not fully engaged; he was yearning for Mannheim and Aloysia—and, indeed, for Italy. Undoubtedly there were several reasons why he refused the appointment of court organist at Versailles—it was a subordinate post, poorly paid, and Grimm was against it—but there was also the feeling that he did not wish to be tied down in France.

Even in his comments on the impending performance of the *Paris* Symphony (No. 31 in D—K. 297), written specially for the *Concert spirituel*, at which it was highly successful, Wolfgang shows his antipathy:

> I cannot say whether it will be popular—and, to tell the truth, I care very little, for who will not like it? I can answer for its pleasing the few intelligent people who will be there—and as for the stupid ones, I shall not consider it a great misfortune if they are not pleased. I still hope, however, that even asses will find something in it to admire—and, moreover, I have been

careful not to neglect *le premier coup d'archet*—and that is quite sufficient. What a fuss the oxen here make of this trick!

Le premier coup d'archet was merely a demonstrative unison opening on the strings, a dashing stroke which any 'hack' could cultivate. Not only in that, but in the prominence given to brilliant string figuration, the plainness of the wind parts, and the willingness to substitute a shorter slow movement at the second performance, the composer did his best to please.

From the outset, Anna Maria cut a lonely figure in Paris. Necessarily left to her own devices for much 'of the time, she tended to sit and knit, and presumably to brood on the dismaying pattern of events in which she was caught up. At first she was far from well, but in May she appeared to recover both physically and in spirit. In mid-June, however, she suddenly became ill. Grimm provided a doctor, but the patient's condition grew steadily worse. On 3 July Anna Maria died, from what cause we do not know. Her son reacted with remarkable composure and good sense—some say callousness—and the same night wrote a warning letter to Leopold preparing him for the worst. (It seems symbolical of Anna Maria's sacrifice that much of this letter is devoted to the success of the *Paris* Symphony.) He then wrote to a family friend, the Abbé Bullinger, asking him to console both father and sister. On 9 July he made known to Leopold the full story.

For Wolfgang, the attempt to conquer Paris was now at an end. Leopold urged him to further efforts, but was himself well advanced with another plan. Both Adlgasser, the court organist at Salzburg, and *Kapellmeister* Lolli had died some months before, and Leopold had embarked on an elaborate diplomatic scheme in the interests of himself and his son. Although, once again, he was not appointed *Kapellmeister*, he secured for Wolfgang the post left vacant by Adlgasser. The archbishop agreed to favourable terms, including freedom to go anywhere to execute a commission for an opera. It is impossible to reconstruct the way this came about, partly because several people at the Salzburg court appear to have been involved, but also because Leopold's account of it is a loaded one directed to persuading Wolfgang to return. Leopold was relying on their prospective combined income for paying off his debts. Even when Wolfgang had reached Munich, where he met up again with Aloysia, Leopold was very anxious. Aloysia, however, had had her head turned by rapid advancement as a singer and was not disposed to attach herself to a penniless Mozart. Perhaps her cold-shouldering finally drove him home. Be that as it may, he arrived at Salzburg on 17 January 1779—and re-entered the service of Colloredo.

THE DEVELOPING
COMPOSER

There was little joy in Wolfgang's return to Salzburg. That there was also little acrimony, which is the more remarkable, says much for the mutual affection of father and son. Not that the relationship could ever again be the same. Leopold had left no doubt that, in his view, Anna Maria's 'needless death in Paris' was a direct consequence of her son's irresponsible behaviour. Wolfgang had stated that he was returning only for his father's sake and that in doing so he was 'committing the greatest folly in the world'. Moreover, he felt that he had been tricked, both by moral pressures and by his father's 'conspiracy' with Grimm to get him started on the journey home. In that there was some truth—and perhaps rather more rationalization.

For the time being, at least, such rationalization was a necessary aid to living with the failures and the follies. The purpose of the journey westwards had been 'to get a good permanent appointment, or, if this should fail, to go off to some big city where large sums of money can be earned' (Leopold), and there was no escaping the fact that nothing had been achieved on either count. The family resources had been used up and, apart from friendship in Mannheim and success with the *Paris* Symphony, little that was agreeable had resulted. Emotionally, Wolfgang had suffered two bitter losses—first his mother, then a sweetheart—and in regard to his mother he cannot have felt entirely guiltless. The depth of his attachment to Aloysia Weber has sometimes been questioned, but it is clear that he had intended making her his wife. Hardly less important emotionally had been the experience of freedom from his father's direct control. The newness of that experience cannot

Idomeneo, Rè di Creta; Stuart Burrows in the title-role, Royal Opera House, Covent Garden, London, 1978. Although infrequently staged, *Idomeneo* is Mozart's greatest opera in the 'serious' or tragic convention and a landmark in his musical development.

73

be overstated, so it is hardly surprising that, at the age of 21 to 22, some follies were committed. Wolfgang must surely have recognized that Leopold's charge of forever building castles in the air had substance; and yet, in this respect, he was to prove incorrigible—or rather, incapable of learning from experience, however painful. Looked at in one way, such wide-eyed optimism is an endearing trait, but there is no denying that much of the hardship of the remaining twelve years or so of the composer's life was to stem from it.

So far as we can tell in the absence of letters, father and son learned to live together again without too many problems. On one level, much must have depended on Nannerl, who will certainly have filled her new role with understanding, imagination and an inner strength. On another, there were problems enough of a more pressing, practical nature: debts that had to be paid, an employer that might well have to be held to his agreement, and always the question of Wolfgang's future. Leopold could not resist occasional reminders that he had been right, and the absence of Anna Maria was a constant symbol of past misdemeanours. For his part, Wolfgang said openly that Salzburg and 'native Salzburgers' were quite intolerable to him. Outwardly, however, he seems to have adjusted reasonably well. Inwardly, creative work provided the best of refuges.

A retrospective look at the music written in Mannheim and in Paris is now desirable. The long-held belief that Mozart had a rooted dislike for the flute is hard to reconcile with the Concerto in G (K. 313), which, as Einstein remarks, 'was written *con amore* from beginning to end'. Surely the dislike concerned certain technical characteristics, not the instrument's expressive qualities. K. 313 and its companion, K. 314—an adaptation of an oboe concerto written shortly before leaving Salzburg—were commissioned by de Jean, a Dutch amateur resident at Mannheim, where Wolfgang also had the stimulus of his flautist friend Wendling. For the same patron he wrote three flute quartets—flute, violin, viola and cello—of which the first, in D (K. 285), is the best. Works of this kind, using a distinctive first instrument, are usually *concertante* chamber music (solo and accompaniment), but parts of K. 285 are indisputably 'pure' chamber music. Eleven years later, in the Clarinet Quintet (K. 581), the *concertante* manner was to be transcended completely.

Works featuring the flute were also written in Paris. The most considerable of these is the Concerto in C (K. 299) for flute and harp, commissioned by the Duc de Guines for himself and his daughter. This is tailored perfectly to both the French taste and the capabilities of accomplished amateurs. The two compositions for the *Concert spirituel*

Early eighteenth-century *opera buffa*; oil painting from the school of Longhi. The simplicity, naturalness and intimacy is in sharp contrast with the grandeur of *opera seria* (compare p. 77). The informal grouping of members of a courtly audience suggests a little two-act entertainment played in the intervals of a three-act *opera seria*. Such were the *intermezzi* of Pergolesi (1710–36), and from these humble beginnings a full-scale comic form developed.

are of quite another stamp. These are Mannheimish in three important respects: the scale of their resources, their musical scope and their sense of public address. The developing composer had experienced Mannheim just in time, for in 1778, when the Duke Karl Theodor inherited Bavaria and moved his court to Munich, the famous orchestra split up, some of its members going with the court, some remaining at Mannheim, and others taking their chance in Paris and elsewhere. Although both the Mozarts were critical of the showier, slicker aspects of the Mannheim style, Wolfgang responded, as always, to the best that he encountered.

The first composition for the *Concert spirituel* was a *sinfonia concertante* in E flat for flute, oboe, horn, bassoon and orchestra. Whether due to muddle or malice is not clear, but plans for the performance in which Wendling and Ramm were to have taken part fell through. Moreover, the score has come down to us only in an arrangement (K. 279b) using oboe and clarinet instead of flute and oboe. Despite the non-performance of this large-scale work—his most ambitious concert item to date— Wolfgang went on to write the *Paris* Symphony: the *Concert spirituel* was a well-established institution and offered the best available platform. As well as seeking to please, the composer seized on the artistic opportunity; never before had he been able to write a symphony for so large an orchestra, with many strings and two clarinets in addition to the usual wind band. The work is designed on a grander scale than any of his previous symphonies, and the way in which it combines the Parisian conventions with inspired imaginative flights is very impressive, especially in the finale. There he contrived a contrapuntal, even fugal, development, but with so light a touch that the music lost none of its 'brilliant' appeal.

The set of six violin sonatas engraved in Paris is interesting in several respects. Known as the Mannheim Sonatas (K. 301–6) because they were dedicated to Maria Elisabeth, the wife of the Duke Karl Theodor, the set was begun in Mannheim and completed in Paris. The creative emulation of a model is emphasized by the fact that in these sonatas the violin and piano participate on more or less equal terms, as distinct from the earlier concept of piano sonatas with violin accompaniment. This approach was prompted by Wolfgang's encounter at Mannheim with the Dresden composer, Joseph Schuster, but unfortunately the Schuster sonatas that so impressed him are quite lost to us. Though keenly exploring the new possibilities, Wolfgang retained the traditional two-movement form that he had learnt from J. C. Bach, the only exception being K. 306, which has three movements. Of special interest is the Sonata in E minor (K. 304), for this is a deeply personal expression, at once keenly felt and superbly controlled. Together with the Piano Sonata in A minor

An *opera seria* in performance at the Teatro Regio, Turin, in 1740; oil painting by Pietro Domenico Oliviero (and collaborators). The architectural grandeur of the set, its scope extended by illusionistic painting, and the pompous posturing on the stage are basic characteristics of this Baroque art form. The orchestra consists of strings, two horns, probably two oboes, two bassoons and two *continuo* units, each made up of harpsichord, cello and double-bass.

76

(K. 310), which was the next work to be written, K. 304 provides striking evidence of a maturing of the composer's powers. Significantly, neither work invites the label *Sturm und Drang*; each is typically Mozartian in both invention and quality of feeling.

By no means all the music from the remaining two years or so at Salzburg reflects this deepening and maturing of Wolfgang's creativity. Some of it is purely 'functional', written to order, perhaps half-heartedly, but still with the finish of a comprehensive master-craftsman and invariably with a personal presence. We do not know why two settings of the *Kyrie* were started and left unfinished, but such fragments (K. 322 and 323) might be thought symbolical of the composer's relationship with the court. Although Colloredo had made concessions, as it seems, and had shown some readiness to reappoint his former *Konzertmeister*, the prevailing climate in the months that followed was one of mutual mistrust. It is not hard to imagine the independent stance adopted by so proud and reluctant a servant. If allowance be made for the difference in generation and in temperament, then Mozart's rebellious-ness at 23 to 24 may be seen as remarkably similar to that of the young Beethoven. How the latter would have sympathized with comments such as this on Salzburg and its court: 'When I play or when works of mine are performed, it is as though the audience consisted of nothing but tables and chairs.' Aristocratic aloofness and a studied indifference were inevitable responses to Mozartian individualism.

One of the first works written after the return to Salzburg was the *Coronation* Mass in C (K. 317). This takes its name from the probability that it was occasioned by the anniversary, on the fifth Sunday after Whitsun, of the crowning of the 'miraculous' image of the Virgin in the church of Maria Plain, north of Salzburg. Be that as it may, K. 317 is a festive mass requiring four soloists as well as choral singers and an orchestra that includes trumpets and drums. Colloredo's views on church music are reflected in the relative shortness, the avoidance of elaborate counterpoint and other 'polytextual' writing (the overlapping, in different voices, of successive sentences of the text), and the inclusion of only one 'aria', a setting for soprano solo of the *Agnus Dei*. But there are also deviations. In that same aria, which is a striking and rapturous anticipation of the Countess's *Dove sono* in *Figaro*, the words are freely repeated for purely musical reasons, and there is much elsewhere that is musically, rather than liturgically, motivated. The *Credo*, for instance, has a symmetrical ground-plan with a centrally placed *Adagio* (*Et incarnatus est*) framed by two matching *Allegro molto* sections: one result is that the music for *Descendit de Coelis* reappears for the closing *Amen*. The two parts of the *Sanctus* (*Sanctus* and *Hosanna*) stand in the

VERA EFFIGIES IMAGINIS B. MARIÆ VIRGINIS CONSOLATRICIS IN PLAIN, MIRACULIS, FAVORIBUS, GRATI-
IS, ET PEREGRINORUM FREQUENTATIONE CELEBRIS, UNA CUM TEMPLO, ALIISQUE TAM SACRIS, QUAM PROPHANIS STRU-
CTURIS ADIACENTIBUS.
1. Imago B. V. Consolatricis. 2. Templum B. V. 3. Contigua habitatio P.P. Benedictinorum. 4. Mons Calvariæ. 5. Ascen-
sus lapideus per Montem Calvariæ, penes ædiculas repræsentantes Mysteria Dominicæ Passionis. 6. S. Sepulchrum Christi.
7. Diversorium peregrinantium. 8. Ædicula lignea, in qua Imago B. V. venerationi primo fuit exposita.

relationship of an introduction and *Allegro* and are thematically related; the *Benedictus* begins orchestrally, in a way that suggests some gay symphonic *Allegretto*—and so on. Both symphonic and operatic techniques are present, and the music is in turn ceremonial, diverting and more obviously liturgical. There is intermittently a more personal vein with unsuspected depths; throughout the many arresting contrasts, the functional and subjective elements are felt to interact—sometimes almost bewilderingly.

The *Coronation* Mass is the 'biggest' of Wolfgang's church compositions from his last years at Salzburg, but in some of the others the subjective element is appreciably more pronounced. The *Vesperae de Dominica* (K. 321), the Mass in C (K. 337) and the *Vesperae solennes de confessore* (K. 339), the last two written in 1780, show a growing lack of

The Wallfahrtskirche (pilgrimage church) of Maria Plain, near Salzburg, for which Mozart is thought to have written his Mass in C (K. 317). This drawing shows the extent of the holy places associated with the cult of the 'miraculous' image of the Virgin, which dates from 1751.

79

concern about deviation from the accepted ecclesiastical usage. The *Benedictus* in K. 337, far from being warm and welcoming, is a severe expression in a minor key and of imposing proportions. In describing this 'most striking and revolutionary movement in all of Mozart's Masses', Einstein goes so far as to use the term 'blasphemous', though perhaps misleadingly: 'aggressively independent' might be nearer the mark. Einstein, however, is valuable in emphasizing the significance of these church compositions in which the personal impulse had become 'so free . . . that it alone would sooner or later have led to a break with the archbishop—for let no one think that Colloredo, who had occasion to hear the works of other masters also, especially Michael Haydn's, was deaf to the subjectivity or musical rebelliousness of his court organist'. No previous writer makes that point.

In the orchestral and instrumental fields, development rather than rebelliousness catches our attention. The most thought-provoking work is the *Sinfonia concertante* in E flat (K. 364) for violin, viola and orchestra, for this impresses upon us that Wolfgang's maturing was as much a human matter as a musical one. Only a deepened awareness of suffering, born of personal experience, can account for the profoundly moving slow movement in C minor. This is not to suggest that the music is consciously (programmatically) 'about' the composer's troubles, past or present. With the exception of some Romantic works—probably fewer than might at first be supposed—great music is not like that; what it expresses or reflects may well have been prompted by some immediate experience but is essentially the composer's capacity for the kind of feeling that is embodied. Whether the feeling be grave or gay, or whatever nameless complex of emotions may be involved, the principle remains the same. For an understanding of Mozart, of all composers, this basic truth cannot be too strongly reaffirmed.

In one respect, K. 364 has a tangible connection with the journey to Paris, for it was at Mannheim that the *sinfonia concertante* was developed. This hybrid form, combining aspects of the Baroque *concerto grosso* with the new symphonic outlook, was cultivated by several of the Mannheim composers, not least Cannabich, whom Wolfgang numbered among his friends. In no comparable work, however, is there so serious a purpose or so high a degree of formal integration. Strictly, the genre is a transitional one—such later examples as Beethoven's Triple Concerto, Op. 56, and Brahms's Double Concerto, Op. 102, are isolated achievements—but there is nothing in the least immature about this work; it takes us to the threshold of Classicism and is one of the first Mozartian masterpieces of indisputable genius. In the outer movements, seriousness and lightness are reconciled; with their sprightly use of oboes and horns, these

Michael Haydn (1737–1806), the younger brother of Joseph Haydn (see p. 113). Apart from Mozart, Michael Haydn was the most distinguished composer in the Salzburg *Kapelle*, which he joined in 1762, and was always respected by Mozart, who modelled his Requiem on one written by Michael Haydn for Archbishop Schrattenbach.

movements have much of the atmosphere of Salzburg serenades, but also a spaciousness and depth. In the *Andante*, the progress from C minor to E flat major and back again—each 'half' is completed with a similar cadence-figure derived from the opening bars—at once defines a perfectly balanced form and encompasses a wealth of heartfelt expression.

The Symphony No. 33 in B flat (K. 319), which was likewise written in 1779, is comparatively lightweight: a typical Salzburg symphony in three movements, scored for strings and pairs of oboes, bassoons and horns, but with much that is distinctively Mozartian. The design of the opening movement is of its time and place, an incomplete sonata form

without repeats and with a thematically independent 'development'. (The latter uses one of Mozart's recurring 'tags': the four-note motive that was ultimately to emerge as the mainspring of the finale of the *Jupiter* Symphony.[13]) The slow movement has a characteristic warmth and inwardness, and exactly in the middle of it—from bar 44, first strings, then winds (*Ex. 1*)— there is one of those moments of linear intensification, brief but poignant, that were becoming so individual a feature of Wolfgang's work. The *buffo* finale is witty and well sustained, and its proportions, with repeats, tend to tilt the balance away from the first movement.

A little later, in Vienna, having added a minuet, the composer revived No. 33 as a 'Viennese' symphony; and he did the same with No. 34 in C (K. 338)— his last Salzburg symphony, written in 1780. This uses trumpets and drums and renews both the scale and the sense of public address achieved in the *Paris* Symphony (No. 31 in D). The opening is a typical expression of Wolfgang's celebratory view of C major, and it is also operatic with specific pointers to *Die Entführung aus dem Serail* (The Abduction from the Seraglio), to be written in Vienna in 1782. The frustrated desire to write such an opera might be said to dominate this symphony, for the music is full of the idioms of *opera buffa*—and, indeed, of the 24-year-old composer's serious operatic intentions. Structurally, the opening *Allegro*, like that of No. 33, invites description as transitional: there are no repeats, and the 'development' is thematically independent. The beginning of the recapitulation, however, remains developmental and renews the minor-key tensions that help to give this movement its distinctive tone and presence. The slow movement is essentially a string piece, but with two viola parts, making possible an added warmth in the middle of the texture. This technique, already used throughout the *Sinfonia concertante* (K. 364), may well have been acquired from Michael Haydn. Here, too, the operatic impulse is strong and the achievement prophetic, for Susanna herself (*Figaro*) is surely within earshot. In the splendidly lithe, athletic finale, Wolfgang's mastery of symphonic activity is brilliantly highlighted by the simplicity of means and an absolute certainty of aim. Musically, the truly Viennese symphonies are felt to lie just ahead.

The small town theatre in Salzburg, used mainly for German plays and operettas, was much frequented by the Mozart family, and Wolfgang found opportunities to write for the travelling companies that visited it. One such work was a small-scale *Singspiel* with a text by Schachtner, the court trumpeter and a family friend. Known to us as *Zaide* (K. 344), this was originally entitled *Das Serail*, which is also the title of the musical play on which it was based. In content, *Zaide* closely foreshadows *Die Entführung*, of which it is the poor relation. Wolfgang intended this 'Turkish operetta'—a popular genre, at once sentimental and moralistic—for performance in Vienna by the company directed by Johann Böhm, an able musician from Munich; but the plan was frustrated by the closure of the theatres following the death of the Empress Maria Theresa, and the music was never quite finished: there is no final number and no overture. An opera overture was invariably the last item to be written.

Also of interest is the incidental music for a Salzburg production of *Thamos, König in Aegypten*, a play by the enlightened nobleman, Tobias von Gebler, whom the Mozarts had met in Vienna seven years before. Both the play and some of the musical symbolism foreshadow *Die Zauberflöte* (*The Magic Flute*), and it has been shown that in the *Thamos* music, written some years before Wolfgang became a freemason, there is already a musical awareness of masonic ideas.[14] Interesting, too, is the arrival of Emanuel Schikaneder as the theatre manager, for it was he who, ten years later, in Vienna, devised *Die Zauberflöte* and commissioned the music. In Salzburg, he soon became a friend of the Mozarts and provided them with free passes for his theatre shows.

During the course of 1780 came the sort of commission that father and son must often have talked about and schemed for. This was from the court at Munich and was for a full-scale *opera seria* to be produced in the next carnival season. The circumstances looked peculiarly favourable. In the first place, since the commission was from his Bavarian neighbour, Karl Theodor, the archbishop was unlikely to make difficulties. Moreover, the libretto had been entrusted to Giambattista Varesco, the court chaplain at Salzburg, which meant that the composer would be

Pietro Metastasio (1698–1782);
oil painting by Pompeo Batoni,
c. 1762. Metastasio, otherwise
known as Trapassi, was the most
renowned Italian librettist of his
age. He acquired immense
operatic authority, and some of
his texts were set to music many
times; *La clemenza di Tito*, for
example, was set by Mozart.

able to keep in touch throughout its preparation. An equally practical
point was the fact that Wolfgang already knew some of the singers
assigned to the principal roles; serious composing could therefore begin
before he travelled to Munich. Perhaps the prospect seemed too good to
be true. No eighteenth-century opera commission was executed without
tribulation.

Italian *opera seria* has been mentioned briefly in Chapter 3. This was
the traditional 'serious' or tragic opera with a history reaching back to
Monteverdi, the first great opera composer, at the beginning of the
seventeenth century. In Mozart's century, *opera seria* had become rigidly
formalized as a succession of recitatives and arias and, outside Italy, was
essentially a court entertainment, even a court ritual. Long after the
comic *opera buffa* had come to be preferred as entertainment, *opera seria*
remained indispensable for the 'great' occasions such as coronations,
weddings and name-days. One of the last examples is Mozart's *La
clemenza di Tito*, written in 1791 for the coronation as King of Bohemia
of the Emperor Leopold II. On that occasion an old libretto by

Metastasio, already set to music many times, was once again resorted to.

It is a strange fact of musical history that, for decades, Metastasio's authority—not to say 'tyranny', which was far greater than that of even the most celebrated singers—held tragic opera firmly in its grip. The reason is that this distinguished man of words had perfected what was felt to be the best form of operatic text. The typical Metastasian libretto made the maximum provision for the art of singing within an orderly framework derived from the principles of the French Classical drama. By 1780, however, both the orderliness (rigidity) and the emphasis on vocal display had brought about a reaction. Indeed, the movement for operatic reform, which ridiculed 'concerts in costume' and pleaded the cause of true drama, had developed in the 1750s; but it was only with Gluck's *Orfeo* (1762) and, still more, his *Alceste* (1767) that practical steps were taken, and these, necessarily, began with Calzabigi, Gluck's librettist. 'I begged him', wrote Calzabigi, 'to banish *i passaggi, le cadenze, i ritornelli* [i.e., purely musical devices] and all the Gothic, barbarous and extravagant things that have been introduced into our music.' And

Contemporary view of the auditorium of the Residenztheater (court theatre) at Munich where *Idomeneo* was first performed.

85

Gluck, for his part, tells us in the famous preface to *Alceste*: 'I tried to remove all the abuses against which good taste and reason have long raised their voices. I believed that I should dedicate the greatest part of my work to aspire to beautiful simplicity and to avoid boasting of artificial devices at the expense of clarity.' In other words, the music must serve the drama. *Alceste* was a major achievement, but strong conservative pressure ensured that many conventional Metastasian operas would still be written. Increasingly, however, and especially when composer and librettist genuinely cared about the drama, compromises were made along Gluckian lines; otherwise, the Munich carnival opera that prompted this digression—*Idomeneo, Rè di Creta* (K. 366)—would not have been the work it is, and our interest in it would be more detached.

With *Idomeneo* Wolfgang was to prove himself, not only a natural man of the theatre, but the greatest dramatic composer of his age. His librettist was inept, both musically and dramatically, and approached the task of reworking in Italian an old French opera book (*Idoménée*, 1712) with self-conscious literary pretension. Far from influencing his work, Wolfgang had very little contact with Varesco; in the later stages, in Munich, when drastic changes had to be made, the two corresponded only indirectly, through Leopold. In specifying particular changes and the reasons for them, the letters to Leopold are very revealing of Wolfgang's dramatic sense; they show a readiness to abandon music as well as words, a capacity for decisive reappraisal in rehearsal—and, significantly, a limit to the concessions made to singers. This last is demonstrated by an episode concerning the composer's friend, the tenor Anton Raaff, for whom the title-role was written. Despite his extensive experience—or perhaps because of it—and certainly without any ill-will, Raaff wanted to be rid of the great quartet in the final act. Wolfgang seems to have handled him gently but firmly:

> He said to me when we were by ourselves: '*You can't let yourself go in it*. It gives me no scope.' As if in a quartet the words should not be spoken much more than sung. That kind of thing he does not understand at all. All I said was: 'My very dear friend, if I knew of one single note which ought to be altered in this quartet, I would alter it at once. But so far there is nothing in my opera with which I am so pleased as with this quartet; and when you have heard it sung in concert, you will talk very differently. I have taken great pains to serve you well in your two arias, I shall do the same with your third one—and shall hope to succeed. But as far as trios and quartets are

Left above: Idomeneo; title page of vocal score, Leipzig, 1797 (?). Although by no means a conventional Metastasian opera, this is still an *opera seria*, and perhaps the latest example that is of lasting interest to opera-goers.

Left, below: Idomeneo, frontispiece for piano score; lithograph by G. Englemann, Paris, 1822. Idamante, son of Idomeneo, King of Crete, welcomes his returning father. But Idomeneo, to placate Neptune and so survive a storm at sea, has vowed to sacrifice the first living creature he meets. In *opera seria* such a conflict between love and duty is the basic theme.

concerned, the composer must have a free hand.' Whereupon he said that he was satisfied. . . .

Posterity has confirmed the composer's judgment. That Act III quartet is a superb example of the 'ensemble of perplexity' in which the principal characters are brought together, on their own musical terms, to illuminate a shared experience; and it is the first Mozartian ensemble of genius.

Because *opera seria* is culturally so remote from us, the greatness of *Idomeneo* is easily underestimated. Compared with *Figaro, Don Giovanni* or *Die Zauberflöte*, productions are few, and yet there is 'a monumental strength and a white heat of passion that we find in this early work of Mozart's and shall never find again': Dent's wise words[15] give exactly the right emphasis. Wherever there were opportunities—for instance, in the substantial provision for a chorus, unusual in an *opera seria*—the composer seized them with creative fire. Throughout the work there is a richness and nobility of expression that owes much to Gluck's example but is Mozartian through and through. If we think of, say, Gluck's Furies, and then consider the musical portrayal of Electra's venom, we shall have some idea of the extent to which Gluck's imagination has been outreached. Once again, Dent's precise observation is well worth quoting:

> Mozart adopts Gluck's declamatory, almost barbarous and unvocal style of phrase, but whereas Gluck's rhythm nearly always becomes monotonous, and his management of purely musical technique often fumbling and helpless, Mozart's complete mastery of symphonic resources enables him to pile up his phrases to a well-defined climax, to contrast the brute force of diatonic harmony with the anguished wail of gliding chromatics.

Another influence, almost certainly, was the more elaborate and varied type of Italian opera that Karl Theodor had known at Mannheim. Significantly, the composer himself described *Idomeneo* as a '*grosse Oper*', not an *opera seria*, and in the earliest published score it is styled *dramma eroico*.

After various problems and delays, *Idomeneo* was first performed on 29 January 1781, two days after Wolfgang's twenty-fifth birthday. Nothing is known of how it went or was received, for as Leopold and Nannerl were present there are no letters. In the days that followed, Wolfgang enjoyed the Munich carnival with abandon, later conceding

88

Christoph Willibald Gluck
(1714–87); engraving by Adlard,
after Joseph Siffred Duplessis,
1775. One of the most
distinguished opera composers of
his generation and ultimately the
most influential. In the best
interests of the drama he
dispensed with the strict
Metastasian conventions and
with musical display as an end in
itself; not until the flood-tide of
Romanticism was his conception
of tragic opera finally outmoded.
Died in Vienna, where Mozart
succeeded him as court
composer.

to his anxious father, 'I put myself in a false light toward you . . . for I
amused myself far too much'. Leopold saw with his own eyes that streak
of 'irresponsibility' which had caused him so much concern when
Wolfgang was at Mannheim.

Leopold's presence at Munich seems to have depended on the
archbishop's departure for Vienna. Indeed, Colloredo's prolonged
absence was exploited by the Mozarts; at the beginning of March they
visited Augsburg, and it must have been there that Wolfgang received
his historic summons to join the archbishop. Whatever form that
summons took, it had the intended effect. On 9 March, Wolfgang was
still at Augsburg, and only six days later he reached Vienna.

VIENNA: MOZART TURNS FREELANCE

The final showdown between the Archbishop of Salzburg and his court organist has been recounted many times, usually with an unhistorical emphasis. To identify so strongly with the underdog that his employer becomes a kind of monster, insensible to the cause of true genius, is to miss the point rather badly. Of course, personalities were a factor, but much more important is the head-on clash of two different views of the artist in society. The archbishop knew very well that that was what it was about, and in his own way so did Leopold, but the embattled Wolfgang needed a villain, which means that he did not see clearly the nature of his situation. He consoled himself with the thought that 'all the nobility in Vienna' were sympathetic towards him and critical of Colloredo; not for one moment, it seems, did he recognize that such 'sympathy' might evaporate when confronted with open rebellion.

From Colloredo's standpoint, the situation was clear-cut. After many demonstrations of superiority and independence, his court organist had extended unilaterally to more than four months the six weeks' leave of absence freely granted for the preparation of *Idomeneo*. So direct a challenge was not to be tolerated; this presumptuous young man must be disciplined—and quickly. It was surely in such a spirit, rather than for purely musical purposes, that Wolfgang was summoned to Vienna. There is circumstantial evidence in the fact that the other two musicians attending the archbishop—the violinist Brunetti and the *castrato* Ceccarelli—were free to live out, whereas Wolfgang was housed in the archbishop's residence. That he was required to eat at the servants' table is strictly unremarkable, but after the freedom and respect enjoyed at

Constanze Mozart, *née* Weber; oil painting by her brother-in-law, Josef Lange, 1782. 'Her whole beauty consists in two little black eyes and a pretty figure': Mozart's comment to his father is strikingly reflected. After many problems with her mother, Constanze became Mozart's wife on 4 August 1782. The ceremony was in St Stephen's Cathedral (see p. 103).

Munich, this token of servitude was bound to be resented bitterly. The description of such mealtimes in a letter to Leopold speaks volumes:

> We lunch about twelve o'clock, unfortunately somewhat early for me. Our party consists of the two valets, that is, the body and soul attendants of His Worship, the *contrôleur*, Herr Zetti, the confectioner, the two cooks, Ceccarelli, Brunetti and—my insignificant self. Note that the two valets sit at the top of the table, but at least I have the honour of being placed above the cooks. Well, I almost believe myself back in Salzburg! A good deal of silly, coarse joking goes on at table, but no one cracks jokes with me, for I never say a word, or, if I have to speak, I always do so with the utmost gravity; and as soon as I have finished my lunch, I get up and go off. We do not meet for supper, but we each receive three ducats—which goes a long way!

Such haughty self-esteem, directed as much at his fellow-sufferers as at his social superiors, was potentially explosive. And how like Leopold, only more so, it all seems! But Leopold would never have rebelled; he would have kept any explosion within himself, and so he soon became alarmed by the tenor of Wolfgang's letters.

The two main burdens of complaint were money and status. The archbishop would not permit his musicians to engage in private enterprise; at first, he even refused Wolfgang permission to play at a charity concert. Moreover, he required their attendance, in an antechamber, whenever he visited the homes of noblemen; they might, or might not, be summoned by a flunkey to enter and perform—to the greater glory of the archbishop. Brunetti and Ceccarelli seem to have accepted this 'antechambering' as a part of the established order, for it was neither new nor uncommon. But they, of course, were not geniuses; more important, in upbringing, experience and self-valuation, they belonged to a different world. The point is made clearly in Wolfgang's account of the archbishop's visit to Prince Galitzin, the Russian ambassador, who remembered the Mozart family from earlier years. To begin with, Wolfgang made his own way there, avoiding the company of his two colleagues, and on arrival conducted himself as an old acquaintance of Galitzin:

> When I went upstairs, Angelbauer [the archbishop's valet] was on hand to tell the lackey to show me up. But I ignored their honours the valet and the lackey, and went straight through

the rooms to the music room, as all the doors were open. And I went straight up to the Prince and paid my respects. Then I stood talking with him. I had forgotten completely about Ceccarelli and Brunetti, for they were nowhere to be seen. They were tucked away behind the orchestra, against the wall, not daring to come forward.

It was on 16 March, the day after reaching Vienna, that Wolfgang made this bold assertion of his human dignity. Since he began as he meant to go on, the only cause for surprise is that nearly two months were to pass before Colloredo rounded on him with 'knave, scoundrel, rascal, dissolute fellow'. In the meantime, he renewed many former acquaintanceships and became ever more persuaded of Vienna's goodwill and of the scope for taking pupils and giving concerts, but was obliged to remain within the constraints of his employment. A less autocratic employer might have been willing to make concessions; but both parties were difficult men, which simply underlines the fact that, ultimately, the two positions were irreconcilable. Indeed, this is further emphasized by the way in which Wolfgang increasingly saw his grievances in terms of personal honour. The extent to which he himself gave offence can only be surmised, for his letters to Leopold, who was extremely anxious, are naturally one-sided. However, there are one or two glimpses—this, for instance, written after the break had been made:

> I ought to have idled away a couple of hours every morning in the antechamber. True, I was often told that I ought to present myself, but I could never remember that this was a part of my duty, and I only turned up punctually whenever the Archbishop sent for me.

Such studied, needling 'forgetfulness', how infuriating it must have been! But there is nothing to be gained from any attempt to apportion blame; far better to recognize in these two determined men the polarization of powerful social forces; the French Revolution was only eight years away. When Wolfgang reflected on Count Arco, who on 8 June had booted him out of the archbishop's residence, he expressed sentiments indistinguishable from those of Beethoven:

> It is the heart that ennobles a man; and though I am no count, yet I have probably more honour in me than many a count. Whether a man be count or valet, the moment he insults me, he is a scoundrel.

That famous kick was received just a month after the effective break (9 May), during which time both Leopold and Arco, who were acting together, had tried in vain to bring Wolfgang back into the fold. Significantly, the point at issue on 9 May had been Wolfgang's failure to comply with an order to return to Salzburg. The difficulties that he made may have been genuine—they look suspicious—but to Colloredo this disobedience was the last straw. Almost certainly, Wolfgang had already decided that his future lay in Vienna, and when Colloredo abused him and told him to get out, he seized the opportunity, making it clear that the pleasure was his. What followed, culminating in the kick, was merely the degrading formality of petitioning for dismissal—complied with, it appears, largely for Leopold's sake.

Leopold had several reasons for anxiety. Not only had his son taken the unthinkable step of openly quarrelling with his princely patron; also he had chosen to lodge with the Weber family, formerly of Mannheim, whose intentions were no less suspect now that Aloysia was married to the actor and painter Josef Lange. There were still the other daughters, notably Constanze, who was 18 and a promising singer: Wolfgang admitted that he enjoyed her company—'I fool about and have fun with her when time permits'—but denied that he was in love or had any thoughts of marriage. Initially, the possibility that Leopold himself might be the object of Colloredo's revenge was a further source of anxiety. Wolfgang insisted that, if the worst were to happen, Leopold and Nannerl should join him in Vienna, where there were good prospects for all three of them.

As so often, the prospects had a rosy hue that is typically Mozartian. The immediate reality proved rather different, for it was summer, the wealthier families had gone into the country and pupils were hard to come by. So there was plenty of time for composition—and for Constanze. Three new violin sonatas were written (K. 376–7 and 380) and were taken up by Artaria and Co., along with three earlier ones to make the usual set of six. There was much composing for the next winter season: sets of variations for use in teaching, a sonata for two pianos (K. 448), the Serenade in E flat (K. 375) for pairs of clarinets, bassoons and horns. . . . This last was intended for the ear of Joseph II, or rather, that of his chamberlain: imperial patronage was to remain an attractive mirage, even though Joseph himself was generally cool and supercilious.

In those first months of freedom there was no lack of euphoria. Summer or no, some musically discerning noblemen were showing a personal interest, not least the Vice-Chancellor, Count Johann Cobenzl, at whose country villa outside Vienna Wolfgang was a welcome guest. There were enough cultivated aristocrats prepared to treat such an artist

The Emperor Joseph II; oil painting by Anton von Maron. He was Holy Roman Emperor, 1765–90, but effective ruler of the Habsburg lands only after the death of his mother, the Empress Maria Theresa, in 1780. His radical reforms, well-intentioned but autocratic, provoked widespread unrest. Genuinely musical, but his approval of Mozart was seldom whole-hearted: 'too many notes, my dear Mozart'.

as a social equal for Wolfgang to be deceived about the consequences of his break with Colloredo. Although rejoicing in his present freedom, he intended, as of old, to seek some worthy court appointment; but the more he 'rose above himself' with men like Cobenzl, the more unreliable he would seem to those kings and princes who might consider employing him. The old order was still unshaken, and so the greater Wolfgang's social success, the more he disqualified himself for traditional relationships. Later, when the French Revolution was an accomplished fact, reservations deepened: Johann Naumann, a minor composer, was not alone in regarding Mozart as 'a musical *sans-culotte*'.

It is interesting to recall the experience of Georg (Jiří) Benda, for many years *Kapellmeister* to the Duke Frederick of Gotha. In 1778, three years before Mozart's rebellion, Benda broke with his patron and tried to establish himself as a freelance musician. He made brief appearances in Hamburg, Paris and Vienna, but was driven by penury to seek another appointment, which he failed to find. By then nearly 60, he abandoned music, withdrew into the country and consoled himself with the works of Voltaire and Rousseau. Benda had made his mark as a composer and had been published by Artaria, so news of him must surely have circulated in Vienna. In a letter to Leopold in 1778, Wolfgang had referred to Benda, whose *Medea* and *Ariadne auf Naxos* (melodramas) had much impressed him, as 'always my favourite among the Lutheran *Kapellmeister*'. Did he come to know of Benda's fate? If so, no reference to it has come down to us.

In December, if not earlier, Wolfgang and Constanze became engaged, which at least gave Leopold the satisfaction of knowing that he had been right all along. That was certainly his only satisfaction. In breaking the news, Wolfgang saw the need, even at nearly 26, to make out the best possible case: his letter of 15 December is a model of sobriety, and Constanze is characterized as a kind-hearted, economical home-maker. Perhaps she was, but nothing could have been better calculated to forestall Leopold's opposition. In the same letter there is a striking example of ruthlessly objective observation:

> She is not ugly, but at the same time far from beautiful. Her whole beauty consists in two little black eyes and a pretty figure. She has no wit, but she has enough common sense to enable her to fulfil her duties as a wife and mother.

Is it objectivity, or simply diplomacy? Portraits of Constanze do indeed bear out the description of her person.

Leopold's mistrust of Frau Weber, now widowed, was amply justified

Schönbrunn Palace, Vienna; oil painting by Bernardo Bellotto, 1759. Mozart first visited this seat of the Habsburgs at the age of six, when he delighted the Emperor Franz I with tricks at the keyboard and kissed the Empress Maria Theresa 'good and thoroughly'. One so young might be freely indulged.

Vienna, view of the Graben, looking towards the Kohlmarkt; coloured engraving by Carl Schütz (nineteenth century). On leaving the Weber household in September 1781, Mozart took a third-floor room in the back of one of these large apartment houses, now Am Graben 8.

by events. Constanze's guardian was brought in and Wolfgang was required to sign a contract promising marriage within three years, the penalty for default being the payment of an annuity of 300 gulden! When her guardian had left, Constanze took the document from her mother and tore it up. The mother's behaviour made further difficulties and in effect brought about an early marriage, which may have been the intention. Meanwhile, Leopold was repeatedly alarmed by gossip picked up in Salzburg.

That winter Muzio Clementi visited Vienna, and on Christmas Eve he and Mozart entertained the court with a piano contest of the kind that Beethoven was to delight in. Of the same generation as Mozart, Clementi made a major contribution, in both composition and performance, to the establishing of an authentic piano style, but imaginatively he was second-rate. In describing the occasion to Leopold, Wolfgang pounced with devastating sureness on the Italian's limitations:

> He is an excellent keyboard-player, but that is all. He has great facility with his right hand. His star passages are thirds. Apart from this, he has not a farthing's worth of taste or feeling; he is a mere *mechanicus*.

As so often when he is commenting on other musicians, the tone is cocky and disdainful; and somewhere in the background is an old family prejudice: 'Like all Italians, Clementi is a charlatan.' Clementi, however, was unsparing in his praise:

> I had never before heard anyone play with such intelligence and grace. I was particularly overcome by an *adagio* and by some of his improvised variations on a theme chosen by the emperor. . . .

According to Wolfgang, the emperor had 'merely wanted to show me off properly to the foreigner' and was 'thoroughly satisfied'. At this stage the prospect of a court appointment in Vienna was a fond illusion. Soon, however, Wolfgang's comments on Joseph II betray a lack of confidence. Already it was clear that Antonio Salieri, who in 1788 was to become *Kapellmeister*, stood high in the emperor's favour. A successful careerist, Salieri at once saw in Mozart a threat to himself and acted accordingly. This may well have a bearing on the stinging words used in reference to Salieri's compatriot. The Clementi episode certainly emphasizes Wolfgang's capacity for 'pulling a long nose'—his own expression. The very qualities that had enabled him to break with Salzburg were now a liability, for they could easily impair the most effective use of his freedom. Except among those with whom he was wholly at ease, his self-esteem was too readily communicated as arrogance. Again one thinks of Beethoven: 'These lordly Viennese, and in particular the emperor, must not imagine that I am on this earth solely for the sake of Vienna.'

That was written in the summer of 1782, against the background of *Die Entführung aus dem Serail*, which was first given on 16 July, almost a year after Gottlieb Stephanie had commissioned it. Stephanie, who admired Mozart's work, was the director of the *Nationalsingspiel*, the short-lived institution founded by Joseph II for the promotion of German opera. There was an excellent cast, and Wolfgang had begun enthusiastically, believing that the work was to be in production that September. But a succession of intrigues and delays—shades of *La finta semplice*!—had brought repeated postponements for fully ten months: this, together with the organized opposition at the first and second performances, is evidence that the composer did not lack enemies.

Die Entführung was immensely successful, both in Vienna and elsewhere; during Mozart's lifetime it was staged more frequently than any other of his operas. The emperor's famous remark—'Too beautiful for our ears, and too many notes, my dear Mozart'—reflects not only his

Muzio Clementi (1752–1832); engraving by Edward Scriven. Pianist, composer and piano manufacturer, he was disparaged by Mozart as 'a mere *mechanicus*', but was generous in his praise of the 'intelligence and grace' of Mozart's playing. His highly successful career in London suggests that Mozart, too, might have solved his problems by settling there.

Antonio Salieri (1750–1825); settled in Vienna in 1766 and succeeded Bonno as imperial *Kapellmeister* in 1788. He considered Mozart a dangerous rival, and at times Mozart was obsessed with Salieri's 'intrigues', but the story that he poisoned Mozart has no foundation. A highly competent second-rater, Salieri had the complete confidence of the Emperor Joseph II.

conservative taste but the newness and richness of the work itself. The average *Singspiel* was a popular play with songs and other musical numbers, closely related to the *opéra comique* and the English ballad opera: a slight enough affair, the music being catchy, serviceable and unpretentious. But in writing *Die Entführung*, Mozart had utilized to the full the excellent resources of the National Theatre; both vocally and orchestrally, this is a score in the grand manner and is arguably too elaborate for the slender text. The plot combines the currently popular 'Turkish' interest—a blend of the exotic and the salacious—with an attempted rescue in the cause of true love and has as its climax the unexpected magnanimity of the mighty Turk. Contrived and stagy it certainly is, but also imbued with the humane values of the Enlightenment. In giving it his elaborate Austro-Italian treatment, the composer may well have been mindful of the fact that the Viennese nobility resented the imposition, by the emperor, of *Singspiel* in place of Italian opera; no doubt his love for Constanze—the heroine bears the same name—was a further stimulus, but most of all he was at last able to write for the theatre the kind of music that he knew to be within him. The 'serious' and the 'comic', the heartfelt and the uproarious, these are blended in a score that abounds in those illuminating shafts that we call Mozartian: beautiful sadnesses that are musically sheer joy; moments of perception that exalt beyond all reasonable expectation. For the mature dramatic personality is already present, the expressive use of the orchestra is epoch-making—and Osmin, the pasha's hatchet-man, remains one of the finest clowns of the lyric stage.

As well as a triumph with *Die Entführung*, July 1782 yielded two major works, both nominally serenades and yet quite different in conception. The first was to a further commission from the Haffner family in Salzburg. Although substantial, this was written hurriedly and sent to Leopold in batches. Later, having set aside the march and a second minuet, Wolfgang added flute and clarinet parts and presented the work as a symphony in D (No. 35, the *Haffner*—K. 385). The other is the strangely intense Serenade in C minor (K. 388) for wind octet. It has been suggested that this was probably written for Prince Alois Liechtenstein— one of the possible employers in view at the time—but there is really no evidence and the origin of the work remains hidden.[16]

Never in the eighteenth century was a serenade less serenade-like. There are four movements, three of them in C minor; the weighty outer movements point towards the piano concerto in the same key (K. 491), and the minuet, so-called, is a remarkable piece of canonic invention, complex, 'learned', and yet suffused with a sensuous charm. The gently lilting *Andante*, in E flat major, is more easily reconciled with the

function of a serenade, yet even this is scarcely social music: the melting suspensions in the principal theme defy the attention of only half an ear; they are full of latent emotion. The coda to the finale (theme and variations) is perhaps the only bit of legitimate serenade music, and the irony is underlined by the inwardness of the last variation. Only a kindred spirit could have been the recipient of such a work.

Kindred spirits there undoubtedly were; musical minds that rejoiced in the passionate seriousness and true feeling of such minor-key music. Perhaps there were rather more of them than Mozart himself supposed. We learn that he was surprised when the C minor *Andante* in his Piano Concerto in E flat (K. 482) was encored. True, this performance was at a subscription concert, and to that extent the audience represented a cultural élite; but such responses should be seen as a corrective to the usual assertions about the 'shallowness' of the Viennese public. There was a fashionable public, but there was also a more discerning one. During his first year in Vienna, Mozart established easy relationships with many of the more cultivated amateurs: Count Cobenzl and Countess Thun, Baron van Swieten, and the lively Baroness Waldstädten.

Baroness Waldstädten was a good keyboard player and a good friend. When Constanze could no longer tolerate living with her mother— Wolfgang had long since moved elsewhere under pressure from

Die Entführung aus dem Serail; Michael Langdon as Osmin and John Fryatt as Pedrillo, English National Opera production, Coliseum, London, 1971. First performed at the National Theatre, Vienna, in 1782, this 'Turkish' *Singspiel* was in Mozart's lifetime his most successful opera.

Leopold—the baroness took her in, and it was there, in a game of forfeits, that a seemingly trifling incident took place which later threatened her engagement. Wolfgang waxed censorious over what he considered an improper frivolity:

> I entreat you, therefore, to ponder and reflect upon the cause of all this unpleasantness, which arose from my being annoyed that you were so impudently inconsiderate as to say to your sisters—and, be it noted, in my presence—that you had let a *chapeau* measure the calves of your legs. No woman who cares for her honour can do such a thing. . . . If it be true that the baroness herself allowed it to be done to her, the case is still quite different, for she is already past her prime and cannot possibly attract any longer—and besides, she is inclined to be promiscuous with her favours.

This letter to Constanze (29 April 1782) outdoes Leopold in earnestness and righteous indignation. It is not easy to interpret. If Wolfgang considered the baroness so corrupt, why did he arrange for Constanze to stay with her? Did he now see the danger of a Weberish light-mindedness in his wife-to-be? One wonders, too, what the background was, for Constanze had reacted strongly to Wolfgang's annoyance and had told him repeatedly that she would have nothing more to do with him. There are many imponderables, and many relevant questions that cannot be answered; so it is easy to read too much into this passing storm.

Three months later, on 4 August, in the face of further problems created by Frau Weber, Wolfgang and Constanze were married. In seeking his father's consent, Wolfgang declared frankly that 'most people' thought they were already man and wife, hence the necessity 'for my own honour and for that of my girl' that they no longer delay. The hurriedly arranged ceremony was in St Stephen's Cathedral, but the wedding party consisted of only five people, including Frau Weber and Constanze's guardian. Afterwards there was a sumptuous feast provided by Baroness Waldstädten. Leopold's reluctant consent was received the following day.

Shotgun marriage or elopement? There would seem to be elements of both. Much depends on whether one believes that Constanze was being housed by the baroness as Wolfgang's mistress. (Such a belief might be thought hard to reconcile with the letter of 29 April.) Frau Weber probably did believe that; she had threatened to have the police fetch her daughter home. But her agreement to the marriage was neither sought nor given, and the couple considered themselves well rid of her.

St Stephen's Cathedral, Vienna, the scene of Mozart's wedding in 1782 and of his funeral service nine years later. In the months before his death Mozart had some assurance of succeeding Leopold Hofmann as the cathedral *Kapellmeister*. In the 1740s both the Haydn brothers were choristers here.

MOZART AND HAYDN

Has any other great musician in his mid–twenties been so completely the product of his upbringing? Perhaps Chopin, and certainly Mendelssohn, but in neither of these cases did a musical father devote 20 years of his life to preparation and supervision. Mozart's ambitions, both musical and social, had been nurtured from early childhood; even his rebelliousness was a natural product of his father's frustrated evaluation of the lords and masters encountered down the years. Contrary to his upbringing, and yet, given his temperament, necessarily a product of it, was the desire for freedom, spontaneity and what Leopold considered idle revelling.

At this stage Leopold seems a melancholy figure. That deep pessimism with which he had regarded so much of Wolfgang's more recent conduct took possession of him. He saw the marriage with Constanze not only as the end of his own effective influence but as the harbinger of still greater follies. To some extent, Wolfgang's habit of presenting his prospects over-optimistically, which was partly his nature and partly an attempt to ease his father's anxiety, made matters worse. On any immediate question, Leopold's judgment was invariably right, and his assessment of Wolfgang's weaknesses was as perceptive as ever. In a letter to, of all people, Baroness Waldstädten—a letter expressing a father's appreciation of her contribution to the wedding—Leopold expands on his son's 'principal fault':

> . . . that he is far too *patient* or rather *easy-going*, too *indolent*, perhaps even too *proud*, in short, that he has the sum total of all those traits which render a man inactive; on the other hand, he

Mozart and Haydn; engraving by A. Benedetti, after Hyacinthe Rigaud. Haydn is shown with a theorbo, much used in the seventeenth and eighteenth centuries as a *continuo* instrument. Amidst the rivalries and intrigues that were so common a feature of the age, the mutual understanding and respect of these two great composers is particularly striking.

is too *impatient*, too *hasty* and will not bide his time. Two opposing elements rule his nature, I mean, there is either too *much* or too *little*, never the golden mean.

It can be shown 'statistically'— that is to say, unsentimentally—that creative genius seldom knows a middle way. Much of the art most valued by posterity has been created in great bursts of activity, wholly single-minded, even recklessly impatient, followed by periods of inertia and frivolity. The history of music is by no means short of examples. Leopold was right in believing that Wolfgang lacked the patience, tenacity and engaging humility demanded by conventional career-making; but he underestimated, if indeed he seriously considered, his son's capability of succeeding as a freelance performer and composer.

Due partly to conditioning, partly to recurring insecurity, Wolfgang never abandoned Leopold's vision of his becoming 'a famous *Kapellmeister*', and yet there must have been times when his life as a freelance seemed much to be preferred, both socially and artistically. At least from the summer of 1782 (*Die Entführung*), the first years in Vienna were highly successful and did not bear out Count Arco's warning: 'A man's reputation here lasts only a short time. . . . After a few months the Viennese want something new.' There was no shortage of worthwhile pupils, and as early as January 1782, having found that young ladies were given to cancelling their lessons, Wolfgang had shown business acumen in changing from payment by the lesson to fixed monthly payments. His mornings were usually devoted to teaching, and often he would lunch with the family, or elsewhere, for there were many invitations, which might mean that it was early evening before there was any chance of sitting down at home to work at composition. 'And frequently I am prevented from doing so by a concert; if there isn't one, I work till nine o'clock.'

Somehow his music got written—or rather, written down. It is well authenticated that Mozart, of all composers, had a rare ability to work at music in his mind, even to the smallest detail, and to retain what he had 'composed'. The rarity is the extent of this faculty rather than the faculty itself. Those who have experienced it invariably tell us that they associate such creation with physical activity, be it walking, shaving or chopping wood. It seems likely, therefore, that the stories of Mozart 'composing' while playing billiards or skittles are essentially true. What is untrue, and wholly unjustified, is the inference that his music always came easily to him. The paucity of laborious sketches and early drafts is merely a pointer—a negative one—to working methods, not evidence of 'divine inspiration' or of any other magical attribute. This needs stressing, because the magical view is very much a part of the Mozart myth. Probably it began with musically innocent people seeing the composer at work, writing fluently and yet attending to their conversation. Some remarks made many years later by Constanze to Vincent Novello, the English composer and music publisher, afford an insight into both the writing out of the music and the state of total absorption in which the real work of composing was done:

> Mozart seldom went to the instrument when he composed. . . . He walked about the room and knew not what was passing around him. When all was arranged in his mind he took inkstand and paper and said: 'Now, dear wife, let's hear what people are talking about.'[17]

The extent of Viennese musical life in the 1780s makes impressive reading. The imperial court and administration, the latter much increased by the new bureaucracy created by Joseph II, and the financial and commercial interests that gravitated to it, to say nothing of the aspirants to office from aristocratic families throughout the Habsburg lands, and all manner of lesser hangers-on, these constituted a sizable public, of whom a significant proportion were musical amateurs. A number of the more influential noble families with palaces or 'town houses' in Vienna were important both as pace-setters and for their own private concerts; and the court itself, despite economies compared with the lavish outlay of earlier times, was still the foremost patron and a prestigious focus.

In his letters to his father, Wolfgang seems to hang on every recognition accorded him by the emperor. For instance, in this description of a concert of his own on 23 March 1783:

> Suffice it to say that the theatre could not have been more crowded and that every box was full. But what pleased me most of all was that His Majesty the Emperor was present and, goodness!—how delighted he was and how he applauded me! It is his custom to send the money to the box-office before going to the theatre; otherwise I should have been fully justified in counting on a larger sum, for really his delight was beyond all bounds. He sent twenty-five ducats. . . .

Clearly, it was time for the emperor to change his custom and pay up afterwards: on a less gratifying occasion, Wolfgang would have said as much—and would have dispensed with 'His Majesty'.

Theater am Kärtnerthor
(Corinthian Gate Theatre),
Vienna, c. 1825. The most
popular of Vienna's theatres and
a familiar scene to Mozart. For a
short time in 1784–5, after the
failure of the *Nationalsingspiel*,
Schikaneder accepted the
Emperor's invitation to promote
German opera here.

That crowded theatre is a scene that was repeated many times, both at Wolfgang's own concerts and at other promotions that included his appearance. Some were joint ventures: for example, the highly successful concerts in the Augartensaal in the summer of 1782, and the four 'grand serenades' in the city squares, both promoted with the young enthusiast Philipp Martin, who was also responsible for weekly concerts of a semi-professional kind. The private 'academies' in such households as those of Prince Galitzin, Count Johann Esterházy and Baron van Swieten were another important field, and there, too, Mozart was much sought after. Moreover, with such cultivated men he enjoyed something like social equality.

Swieten's Sunday concerts are of particular interest because they were devoted to 'old' music—Baroque, with some Renaissance—and were responsible for the enlargement of Mozart's resources through the 'discovery' of J. S. Bach. The immediate result was not only an outbreak of fugues—notably the one in C minor for two pianos (K. 426), later to

be arranged for strings with an introductory *Adagio* (K. 546)—but also a number of works in which other aspects of Baroque expression were creatively renewed: the Sonata in A (K. 402) for violin and piano, the *Adagio* in C minor (K. 396) and the Fantasia in D minor (K. 397), both for the piano, and most of all, the Mass in C minor (K. 427). Three of these, including the Mass, were left unfinished. Perhaps this indicates misgivings about Baroque techniques imitated rather than assimilated: compare, for example, the fugal finales in Haydn's *Sun* Quartets. For Mozart, as for Haydn, true assimilation was to mean a more flexible and independent use of imitative counterpoint. Einstein, however, finds it significant that all these unfinished works were in some sense written for Constanze, and that Wolfgang 'never finished any of the compositions intended for her', the implication being that he was dispirited by her limited, even pretended, musicality.

Whatever the truth may be, it is strange that the C minor Mass remained unfinished, for this was begun in fulfilment of a vow—a

Vienna, the old Burgtheater, which under Joseph II became the National Theatre; coloured engraving by Karl Postl. It was here that *Die Entführung aus dem Serail, Le nozze di Figaro* and *Così fan tutte* were first staged.

promise 'in my heart of hearts'—and was intended for performance at Salzburg when the newly married couple first visited Leopold and Nannerl. For various reasons, that visit did not take place until the summer of 1783, by which time the Mass had been awaiting completion for more than six months. It is believed, though scarcely proven, that a performance was given in the Peterskirche, Salzburg, on 25 August, and that Constanze was one of the two soprano soloists. If so, it would seem that some earlier *Credo* and *Agnus Dei*, despite differences in style and scale of treatment, must have been incorporated.

Apart from the Requiem, which was commissioned, the Mass in C minor is Mozart's only major work to a liturgical text after his break with Salzburg, and it is the greatest of all his church compositions. This is a large-scale cantata mass in the tradition of Haydn's *St Cecilia* Mass and Bach's *Mass in B minor*, which means that the treatment of the text has been determined by musical rather than liturgical needs. In this and other respects, the work is a counterblast to the church music reforms associated with Colloredo and Joseph II—'true church music', noted Wolfgang, 'lies in attics, almost eaten by worms'—as well as a reflection of enthusiasms engendered by Swieten. The most elaborate section is the *Gloria*, which falls into seven self-contained movements. These include a

Baron Gottfried van Swieten, president of the Education and Censorship Commission and librarian of the Court Library; engraving by Mansfeld, after J. C. de Lakner. Swieten had served as ambassador to the Prussian court and had returned with a missionary enthusiasm for the music of J. S. Bach and Handel. His zeal in promoting 'old' music made him the most influential of the Viennese amateurs. Both Mozart and Haydn were indebted to him.

choral opening closer to Handel than to Bach, a *galant* number with a coloratura soprano solo (*Laudamus te*), a gravely powerful *Qui tollis* in G minor that has the flowing lines of a double chorus pitted against a jagged Baroque rhythm on the orchestra, and a strenuous choral fugue for *Cum sancto spiritu*. There is much that is knowingly archaic: the operatic work that comes to mind is *Idomeneo*. Not until the late masses of Haydn, written several years after Mozart's death, was such archaism fully reconciled with the symphonic outlook.

The visit to Salzburg was not a success. There was no open clash, so far as we know, but Leopold's welcome was qualified, his acceptance of Constanze rather coldly polite, and Nannerl seems to have behaved similarly. Wolfgang was in no doubt that Constanze was considered unworthy of him. In so far as it is possible to weigh such matters, Leopold was right, for Constanze was uneducated, and neither in awareness nor sensibility could she begin to match her husband. Moreover, comparisons with Nannerl must surely have been made. Still, they stayed from early August until the end of October, and many friends and acquaintances were visited. One such was Michael Haydn, who was far from well and under pressure from the archbishop for the completion of some music. So Wolfgang went again to Michael's

Linz; engraving by Joseph and Peter Schaffer, *c.* 1790. Mozart first visited Linz in 1762 and then again in 1783, when he gave a concert for which the *Linz* Symphony was written.

house—hard against the Mönchsberg, this is now the booking-hall for the funicular railway to the castle—and wrote for him two string duos (K. 423 and 424), which were duly passed to Colloredo as Haydn's work. Also visiting Salzburg at that time was the blind pianist Maria Theresa Paradis, for whom the Piano Concerto in B flat (K. 456) was written in the following year.

The Mozarts' journey home was by way of Linz, where they were the guests of 'old Count Thun' and the *Linz* Symphony (No. 36 in C – K. 425) was written hurriedly for a concert at the town theatre. If there is any evidence of hurry, it is in the use of well-tried formulae for C major brightness—compare with Symphony No. 34—but such a notion is immediately countered by the freshness and vitality. This is a fully-fledged Viennese symphony—there is even a slow introduction—and contains many distinctive ideas, nearly all of which speak to us of *opera buffa*, or rather, of what Mozart was to make of it. The slow movement (*Poco Adagio*) is the most affecting, and most concentrated, in any of his symphonies so far and takes us close to that of the *Prague* Symphony, written three years later.

On reaching Vienna, Wolfgang and Constanze learnt that their first-born, a son, had died in their absence. The baby was little more than a month old when they had left him in the care of some sort of infants' home—descriptions vary—and had set out for Salzburg. This incident seems to symbolize the precariousness of so much in their nine years of domestic life. The circumstances in which they lived would have made demands on the most orderly of households, which theirs was not. First, they were frequently on the move: by the time the first baby was born (June 1783), they had already changed lodgings three times. Often, a move to better or poorer accommodation seems to have reflected the immediate state of Wolfgang's finances. Secondly, by living up to, or beyond, a fluctuating income, they made it inevitable that money problems were always with them. These were aggravated by errors of professional judgment. As early as February 1783, having taken out a loan in order to market three piano concertos (K. 413–5) on a subscription basis, Wolfgang had to appeal to Baroness Waldstädten:

> . . . if I do not repay the sum before to-morrow, he will bring an action against me. . . . At the moment, I cannot pay—not even half the sum! If I could have foreseen that the subscriptions for my concertos would come in so slowly, I should have raised the money on a longer time-limit. I entreat your Ladyship for Heaven's sake to help me to keep my honour and my good name!

Joseph Haydn (1732–1809); oil painting by Thomas Hardy, London, 1791. The foremost innovator of his generation—Einstein calls him 'one of the great men against their time'—Haydn did more than any other composer to bring the sonata style to its Classical maturity. Mozart was deeply influenced by him, and he, in turn, responded creatively to Mozart.

'If I could have foreseen . . .': such foresight was not in Wolfgang's nature; unreal hopes and over-optimism certainly were. (On this occasion, Leopold had suggested that six ducats was too high a price for the concertos.) Thirdly, Constanze's pregnancies imposed an ever-recurring burden: in eight years, six children were born, but only two, both boys, survived infancy. The undermining of Constanze's health was to prove a further complication.

It must not be supposed that these stresses added up to a life of unhappiness. Nor is there evidence that Constanze was, as some have said, extravagant or inept as a housewife. The casual opportunism derived from her upbringing enabled her to fall in readily enough with Wolfgang's spontaneity, irregular hours and zest for living. Despite all the pressures, they enjoyed an active social life, entertaining, visiting and joining in the festivities that each season brought. For instance, during the carnival of 1783, Wolfgang put on a pantomime with himself as Harlequin, Aloysia Lange as Columbine and her husband as Pierrot, and together with Constanze gave a private ball which lasted until seven in the morning. In 1785, Leopold stayed with his son and daughter-in-law for about two months, and he sent Nannerl this heartfelt impression of the bustle of their lives:

> We never go to bed before one o'clock and I never get up before nine. We lunch at two or half past. The weather is horrible. Every day there are concerts; and the whole time is given up to teaching, music, composing and so forth. I feel rather out of it all. If only the concerts were over! It is impossible for me to describe the rush and bustle. Since my arrival your brother's fortepiano has been taken at least a dozen times to the theatre or to some other house.

It is inconceivable that Constanze could have fully understood the nature of Wolfgang's genius. Perhaps it was as well for her peace of mind that she could not. But she knew that he had a power within him and that it was important. Beyond that she seldom ventured. In this respect, Wolfgang was realistic; the fact that his wife was hardly a soul-mate seems to have bothered him much less than it has bothered posterity. The assumption that a soul-mate is what a great artist most needs is a Romantic one: the Mozarts' marriage knew none of the storms that that sort can bring. Here was a warm domesticity with a strong bond of physical attraction; a marriage that was a function of the ordinariness of the man, not of the artist's uniqueness. On the whole, it worked very well.

The Empress Maria Theresa; oil painting by an unknown artist, Vienna, probably c. 1765. Maria Theresa ruled the Habsburg lands for 40 years, and her death in 1780 marked the end of an era. The Josephine age, which followed, commended itself to men of the Enlightenment, but the passing of Maria Theresa's traditionalism was regretted by many.

Karl Ditters von Dittersdorf (1739–99). Of the same generation as Haydn, he was a prolific composer for Vienna and for various noble patrons. His *Doktor und Apotheker* is still occasionally revived in German opera-houses, but little of his music is generally known. In Vienna he played string quartets with Haydn, Mozart and Vaňhal.

Despite the sense of tumult, which undoubtedly wore him down, Leopold's visit in 1785 brought him much happiness. In the previous summer, Nannerl had married and had gone to live at St Gilgen, so Leopold was now quite alone. There must have been several respects in which his winter journey to Vienna was undertaken with misgiving, but much of the earlier rapport between father and son was regained, though necessarily with a difference. Leopold witnessed some of Wolfgang's greatest concert successes, including the first performance of the Piano Concerto in D minor (K. 466), which impressed him immensely; many old friends and acquaintances sought him out, invariably with glowing tributes to his son, and almost every day there were social engagements. A number of his former judgments had to be revised, and he even found a good word to say for Frau Weber, whose dinner in his honour was 'excellently prepared'.

Some knowledge of the discussions between Leopold and Wolfgang would be invaluable: on freemasonry, for example. About a year before, Wolfgang had become actively involved in this progressive movement, and he had already written his first masonic composition, the cantata *Dir, Seele des Weltalls* (To Thee, Mind of the Universe, K. 429). Shortly after Leopold's arrival in Vienna, Haydn became a member of the same lodge—*Zur wahren Eintracht* (True Concord)—and in April, just before his departure, Leopold himself entered the order. The 1780s were the golden age of Viennese freemasonry; the ideals of reason, virtue and human brotherhood attracted many of the noblest minds, and the most active members, because of their liberal tenets, were often held to be subversive of 'good order'. The Church was hostile, but the Mozarts, Haydn and many others reconciled their freemasonry with Catholicism. Maria Theresa had suppressed the order, and Karl Theodor did likewise in 1784. Joseph II showed an equivocal sympathy, but when he died in 1790, the Church led a successful campaign of vilification: to be a freemason in the Revolutionary period was tantamount to being a Jacobin.

Mozart's masonic commitment is discussed in Chapter 11, in connection with *Die Zauberflöte*. Meanwhile, it is tempting to ask whether that commitment influenced Haydn's decision to enter the order. Unfortunately, the friendship of Mozart and Haydn is to a large extent submerged, for there is little documentary material. In the letters to Leopold, Haydn is seldom mentioned, and yet, together with two other Viennese composers, Karl Ditters von Dittersdorf and Jan Vaňhal, Haydn and Mozart met repeatedly, often in the latter's home, to play string quartets. Their mutual respect and admiration was boundless, and to no other composer was the mature Mozart so deeply indebted. The

116

creative impact of Haydn's string quartets Opp. 17 and 20 has already been noted, and that of his Op. 33 quartets was greater still.

Haydn's Op. 33 (1781) is a prominent landmark at the beginning of the Classical period. In claiming that these six quartets were written in an 'entirely new and special manner', the composer can only have been referring to the close working of thematic ideas—short motives, in fact—with a wealth of interplay between the parts. Although not strictly new, this technique is used more richly and consistently than before and with a mature mastery of large-scale organization. Mozart was so impressed that he made an exhaustive study of Op. 33 and in the following year began writing a set of six quartets which he dedicated to Haydn in the warmest and most generous terms:

> . . . Most celebrated man and my very dear friend, take these six children of mine. They are, indeed, the fruit of long and laborious toil. . . . During your last stay in this capital, you yourself, my very dear friend, expressed your pleasure in these compositions. Your approval encourages me to offer them to you and leads me to hope that you will not find them wholly unworthy of your favour. Please receive them kindly and be a father, guide and friend to them!

These quartets (K. 387, 421, 428, 458, 464 and 465) were written over a period of about two and half years, between 1782 and 1785: full weight should be given to 'long and laborious toil', not because the music is 'laborious', which it is not, but because the achievement, in almost every movement, is so individually distinguished. The scale, the richness of expression, the close motivic working, these and other aspects show the reality of the debt to Haydn. No less striking, however, is Mozart's personal presence—his feline elegance and subtlety, liking for chromaticism and feeling for major-key pathos—to say nothing of the absence of Haydn's sense of the open air. There are few surprises in formal design: Haydn's *fausse reprise* and the unexpected twists in his recapitulations are largely foreign to Mozart, whose ground-plans tend to be more regular, more predictable. (This is generally true of the orchestral works as well as the chamber music, but not of the piano concertos nor the string quintets—see Chapter 9.) On the other hand, the harmony is often more adventurous than Haydn's, the polyphonic texture more subtle, and a characteristic chromaticism creates a disturbing inner tension: qualities that go far to explain the reservations expressed by contemporary critics. In January 1787, the Vienna correspondent of the *Magazin der Musik* reported sadly:

He is the best and cleverest pianist I have ever heard; but it is a pity that in his ingenious and really beautiful compositions he goes too far in his attempt to be new, so that feeling and sentiment are little cared for. His new quartets, dedicated to Haydn, are too strongly spiced—and what palate can stand that for long?[18]

'Too strongly spiced', 'too many notes': from now on, a recurring commentary on Mozart's music, which means a growing recognition, and rejection, of an important fact about that music: namely, that much of it defies acceptance merely as a cultivated diversion. Significantly, these superb examples of the new chamber music, written, not to order or to satisfy a ready market, but for their own sake, proved to be the parting of the ways. Consider, for instance, the finale of the Quartet in G (K. 387), which combines fugal counterpoint with passages of the plainest homophony, thereby foreshadowing the finale of the *Jupiter* Symphony; or the deeply expressive *Adagio* from the *Hunt* Quartet in B flat (K. 458); or the sheer intensity of the introduction to the *Dissonance* Quartet in C (K. 465): three examples of the kind of music that troubled conventional 'palates'. One wonders, too, what Leopold Mozart made of such music. The *Hunt*, the *Dissonance* and the A major (K. 464)—the last three in the set—were heard by Leopold on the day after his arrival in Vienna, and it was then that Haydn made his celebrated declaration: 'I tell you before God, and as an honest man, that your son is the greatest composer I know, either personally or by name; he has taste and, moreover, the most profound knowledge of composition.'

'Taste' and 'knowledge' were the two essential prerequisites for any artist in the eighteenth century. But the concepts themselves were not absolute: what Haydn considered Mozart's taste, some others heard as extravagance, and the knowledge that Haydn had in mind was not the same as that of the pedants. For some 25 years, Haydn had been a seeker after 'knowledge of composition' and, because of his keenness for trying new ways, had not only acquired but had created knowledge. By progressively integrating elements from different aspects of the *galant* style, the *Sturm und Drang* and other sources, and at the same time deepening his understanding of how to structure music dramatically by means of key-tension and its resolution, Haydn did more than any other composer to bring the Classical style into being. What he recognized in Mozart's new quartets was the seriousness and depth of a fellow-worker who, although his junior by 24 years, was in some respects already moving ahead of him.

The Viennese Classical style is one of the most distinctive and

comprehensive achievements in European musical history. Its comprehensiveness consists in the power of unifying all manner of contrasts within dynamic forms rendered stable by internal balances, not least in matters of key. When Tovey remarks on 'all that variety of colour and rhythm and continual increase of breadth which is one of the most unapproachable powers of the true classics',[19] he is drawing attention to one of the most important capabilities of the Classical style, that of expansion. But concentration is also of its nature and is compatible with expansion. Moreover, like everything else that animates the Classical forms, both these capabilities are in essence dynamic; and yet a sense of underlying composure, of wholeness, of objective order is no less fundamental to the listener's experience. Such paradoxes are at one with the emotional complexity of the music, which is itself indicative of the progressive (bourgeois) content of Classicism, however aristocratic the social ambience in which the style developed. To put it another way, Classicism is the ultimate expression in music of the spirit of the Enlightenment: an inescapable perspective as we follow Mozart into the later 1780s.

L'Assemblée au concert; engraving by François Nicolas Barthélemy Dequevauviller (1745–1807) after Niklas Lafrensen (1737–1807). Almost certainly, the musicians include both professionals—the instrumentalists on the right?—and aristocratic amateurs. Much string quartet playing was likewise by socially 'mixed' ensembles.

119

OPERATIC MASTERPIECES

Despite the successful concert work and the writing of string quartets and piano concertos of great distinction, Mozart's innermost yearning was still for the opera-house. Between *Die Entführung* and *Figaro* there was much talk of operatic projects. In 1783, work was begun on *L'oca del Cairo* (The Goose of Cairo, K. 422), but this was soon abandoned, and *Lo sposo deluso* (The Deceived Husband, K. 430) fared similarly. We cannot be sure why these were not completed, but as they were not commissioned works, dissatisfaction with the dramatic subject matter or with its treatment might be suggested as a possible reason. This is purely speculative, but in the light of *Figaro* and *Don Giovanni* not unlikely. Each of these four works is an Italian *opera buffa,* the genre that dominated the Viennese stage in the middle and later 1780s, but *Figaro* and *Don Giovanni*, quite apart from their accomplishment, are no ordinary examples: in a word, they are much more serious.

Mozart's seriousness is in no way incompatible with either his sense of fun or his mastery of the *buffo* style. It is a serious concern with people, and in particular with personal and social relationships: real people, not the stock figures of a conventional *opera buffa*. 'Serious' opera, however, was even further removed from reality and was bound up with the cultural myths of the aristocracy and the courts. Even *Idomeneo* belongs to that Baroque version of antiquity in which rulers' problems are resolved by gods and oracles, and it seems significant that the great ensemble in Act III uses a mode of expression borrowed from *opera buffa*—the 'ensemble of perplexity'. For such an ensemble, in which the principal characters are brought together, on their own musical terms, to

Don Giovanni; as the Don makes his escape, Leporello 'consoles' Donna Elvira with a catalogue of his master's conquests: from a series of eight engravings, after J. H. Ramberg, Leipzig, 1825. Leporello's aria, 'Madamina' (Act I, Scene 5), is one of the finest for a bass in the entire repertory of *opera buffa*.

Giovanni Paisiello (1740–1816); engraving, after Elizabeth Vigée-Lebrun. One of the most distinguished composers of *opera buffa*, he was best known for his *Barbiere di Siviglia*, which preceded Rossini's by 34 years. Mozart met Paisiello in Naples, in 1770, and again in Vienna, in 1784; he liked both the man and his music.

Lorenzo da Ponte (1749–1838); engraving by Michele Pekenino, after Nathaniel Rogers. Originally Emmanuel Conegliano—his father was an Italian Jewish artisan—Da Ponte lived a varied and adventurous life, eventually settling in New York, where he died. Came to Vienna in 1781, and in 1784 was appointed poet to the imperial theatres; Mozart's librettist for *Le nozze di Figaro, Don Giovanni* and *Così fan tutte*.

illuminate a shared experience, presupposes a complex view of human relationships that is 'modern', not Baroque.

Mozart developed ensemble-writing beyond anything that he knew in the music around him, and he did so within a framework provided by the comic, or popular, genres, notably *opera buffa*. By the 1780s, *opera buffa*, which was popular in origin, had tended to become stereotyped both musically and in the sameness of its plots, but its tradition of debunking the high and mighty was very much alive. The most typical plots centred on a servant-and-master relationship in which the 'humble' servant outwitted his or her bumbling superior: from Pergolesi's *La serva padrona* (The Maid as Mistress, 1733), which is the best known of the earlier *buffo* works, to Mozart's *Figaro* (1786) the line of continuity is unbroken, but the development in scale and scope is immense. Musically, *opera buffa* has a 'naturalness' in keeping with its plots. Although the basic pattern of recitative and aria derives from *opera seria*, the recitatives are more speech-like, the arias less elaborately stylized; there is no place for vocal gymnastics, or for the *castrato* voice, and popular idioms abound.

The composer who comes closest to Mozart in this genre is Giovanni Paisiello, whose masterpiece, *Il barbiere di Siviglia* (1782), was perhaps the most successful of all such works—until supplanted by Rossini's *Barbiere* (1816). In 1784, Mozart met Paisiello, whom he liked, and who shared his progressive views; he certainly knew Paisiello's *Barbiere*, and this may well have played a part in prompting the choice of Beaumarchais's *Le Mariage de Figaro* as material for an opera. Another possibility is that the idea came from Schikaneder, whose German translation of the play had recently been rejected in Vienna. Whatever the prompting, *Figaro* was Mozart's project, not his librettist's, but whether it would have come to fruition or have been performed if the librettist had been other than Da Ponte is open to question.

Lorenzo Da Ponte was a worldly priest, a poetic adventurer with good literary connections, and he proved to be by far the best librettist that Mozart worked with. It was a happy collaboration, much in contrast with the poet's previous experience with Salieri. Moreover, despite his sympathy with Mozart's attitude to authority, Da Ponte had the ear of Joseph II and personally overcame the emperor's objections, partly by omitting Beaumarchais's more inflammatory passages—the most important is Figaro's political diatribe in Act 5[20]—and partly by sheer diplomacy. When the opera was first given, the play was still banned as politically subversive.

What, then, were Mozart's and Da Ponte's intentions? Is *Le nozze di Figaro* (K. 492) in any sense a revolutionary work? These questions

require clear-headedness, for so many claims and counter-claims have been made. Certainly there is nothing revolutionary about the form or the expressive means. In so far as there are innovations, which is not far at all, these are of the kind that enriches rather than transforms: the extensions of dramatic conversation, for instance, and the added importance given to the orchestra. But to regard *Figaro* simply as the richest and most perfect example of third-stage *opera buffa* would be both unimaginative and historically inept.

As has already been suggested, the relationship between Figaro and Count Almaviva marks the culmination of a tradition reaching back half a century and more; but the characterization, in both the text and the music, is quite another matter. This has everything to do with Mozart's, and Da Ponte's, seriousness. The traditional *buffo* manner is closely related to the *commedia dell'arte*. However near the social knuckle, it is, in a sense, licensed jesting. In *La serva padrona*, for example, we do not take Serpina and Uberto seriously; they are meaningful types, but they belong to the stage and are bounded by it. But if we fail to take Figaro and the Count seriously, as real human beings, individualized and drawn from life, to say nothing of Susanna and the Countess, then there is something wrong with the production or with us. Here is no mere stage confrontation, and the greatest disservice we can do this opera is to imagine that it is set in some theatrical dreamland. *Figaro* is of Mozart's own world, the world of Colloredo, Arco and their like. The Count and the Countess are as real as their equivalents in those eighteenth-century audiences for which the work was written. It was a true confrontation, across the orchestra pit. The characterization is deeper and richer than that of Beaumarchais: for instance, the two arias for the Countess, which make her so human and sympathetic a study, have no counterparts in the play. In the new 'democracy' of Mozart's opera, the essential humanity of each individual, whether nobleman or serving-maid, receives the same thoughtful scrutiny. Properly considered, this may well be deemed more deeply revolutionary than any aspect of the play. There is no more central achievement of the Enlightenment in music.

In terms of practical experience, *Figaro* is much indebted to *Die Entführung*. The main development is in the extent to which dramatic conversation is used, and this begins with the libretto. Mozart's responsiveness is shown magnificently in the act finales, but by no means there alone, for duets and trios are a notable feature. The formal aria, treated as a soliloquy, has less than its traditional prominence. In Act I, for example, we come to know Susanna through her part in three duets and a trio; not until she disguises Cherubino in Act II does she have an aria (*Venite inginocchiatevi*): an aria, but not a soliloquy, for she busily addresses Cherubino and the Countess. Where we do find arias that are soliloquies, their inwardness is often peculiarly poignant: Cherubino's *Non so più*—in effect a soliloquy, despite Susanna's presence—and the Countess's *Porgi amor* and *Dove sono* are the foremost examples. There is both variety and subtlety in the shaping of the arias. In several instances the subtlety is a matter of appropriateness, and nowhere more so than in Figaro's *Se vuol bellare, signor Contino* early in Act I. This is a modified version of the old *da capo* aria, the mainstay of the unreformed *opera seria* associated with the courts. The appropriateness is satirical: Figaro is pledging himself to outwit the Count—'You may go dancing, but I'll play the tune'—and he does so in a gentle minuet rhythm (*Allegretto*) with a tune that is mockingly gracious. When this opening section returns, the satirical effect is greater still, for in the second section (*Presto* in 2/4 time) it is clear that the Count will be made to dance to a livelier tune. Although written under great pressure, *Figaro* is rich in musical subtleties.

After intrigues involving Salieri and Righini, each of whom had an opera at the ready, *Figaro* was put into rehearsal at the command of the emperor and was first performed, at the National Theatre, on 1 May 1786. So enthusiastic were the first two audiences that encores were subsequently forbidden, though with little success. Nonetheless, there were only nine performances, and *Figaro* was soon overshadowed by both Dittersdorf's *Doktor und Apotheker*, produced in July, and Vicente Martín y Soler's *Una cosa rara*, which appeared in November. Martín y Soler, an Italianate Spaniard, was one of the most successful composers of *opera buffa*, but is now remembered only by name: Dent dismisses his music as 'empty and commonplace' and notes his 'facility for writing amiable melodies in 6/8 rhythm'. *Figaro* was not revived in Vienna for two years.

One of the principals in *Figaro*—he sang Don Basilio—was the Irish tenor Michael Kelly, who much admired Mozart and was a good friend. To him we owe not only a first-hand account of the preparation of *Figaro* but also some rare glimpses of Mozart himself:

> He was a remarkably small man, very thin and pale, with a profusion of fine fair hair, of which he was rather vain. He gave me a cordial invitation to his house. . . . He always received me with kindness and hospitality. He was remarkably fond of punch, of which beverage I have seen him take copious draughts. He was also fond of billiards and had an excellent billiard table in his house. Many and many a game have I played with him, but always came off second best. . . . He was

Michael Kelly (1762–1826);
mezzotint by Charles Turner
after James Lonsdale. After
singing in operas throughout
Italy, this Irish tenor and
composer was engaged by the
National Theatre in Vienna,
where he created the roles of
Don Basilio and Don Curzio in
Le nozze di Figaro. He was also a
good friend to Mozart: see
bibliography.

kind-hearted and always ready to oblige; but so very
particular, when he played, that if the slightest noise were
made, he instantly left off.[21]

Some of Kelly's comments on *Figaro* leave a vivid impression of
Mozart's involvement and of his ability to involve others:

All the original performers had the advantage of the
instruction of the composer, who transfused into their minds
his inspired meaning. I shall never forget his little animated
countenance, when lighted up with the glowing rays of
genius;—it is as impossible to describe it as it would be to paint
sunbeams.

Two other good friends in the mid-1780s were Stephen Storace, who
was one of Mozart's composition pupils, and his sister Nancy. Some of
the quartet parties with Haydn, Dittersdorf and Vaňhal took place in the
Storaces' home, and Nancy Storace, who was Italian-trained, was the
original Susanna. Nancy was only 19, a natural beauty and a highly
accomplished singer; she had the graces and the artistic sensibility that
Constanze lacked, and it is clear that Wolfgang was greatly attracted to
her. What their relationship amounted to we do not know, but after
Wolfgang's death, Nancy did not comply with Constanze's request for
the return of his letters. The *scena* and aria (K. 505) written for her is
rightly described by Einstein as 'a declaration of love in music'.

It was in the aftermath of *Figaro* that another English composition
pupil, Thomas Attwood, suggested a visit to London. Had it come
about, this visit would have been made in the company of Kelly and the
Storaces, but a part of the plan was for Leopold to take charge of the two
young children. 'Not at all a bad arrangement!' exclaimed Leopold in a
letter to Nannerl. 'They [Wolfgang and Constanze] could go off and
travel—they might even die—or remain in England—and I should have
to run after them with the children.' Poor Leopold; his letter to
Wolfgang is not extant, but we learn that it was 'very emphatic': 'If he
cares to do so, he will find my excuse very clear and instructive.' From a
number of letters to Nannerl it is clear that the relationship between
father and son, so much improved during Leopold's visit to Vienna, had
once again deteriorated. The London project was dropped, and instead
preparations were begun for another winter season in Vienna.

The year 1786 was one of the most richly productive. Alongside
Figaro, Mozart wrote two of his greatest piano concertos—No. 23 in A
(K. 488) and No. 24 in C minor (K. 491)—and in December he added

another, No. 25 in C (K. 503). These are discussed in the next chapter. A small *Singspiel*, *Der Schauspieldirektor* (The Impresario, K. 486), was produced quickly for performance in the orangery at Schönbrunn, and there were several chamber works of striking individuality: the Piano Quartet in E flat (K. 493), which, together with the one in G minor (K. 478), elicited from the publisher Franz Hoffmeister an exhortation to 'write more popularly'—more superficially, that is; the *Hoffmeister* Quartet in D (K. 499), said to have been written in payment of a debt to the publisher, but deeply individual; two piano trios (K. 496 and 502) and the Trio in E flat (K. 498) for clarinet, viola and piano. In December came the Symphony No. 38 in D (*Prague*—K. 504), which was completed just two days after the C major Concerto. The clarinet trio and the symphony call for further comment.

The so-called *Kegelstatt* (skittle-alley) Trio takes us into the family circle of Gottfried von Jacquin, who was one of Wolfgang's closest friends and whose sister, Franziska, was a favourite piano pupil. The piano part was written for Franziska, the clarinet part almost certainly for Anton Stadler, who was later to receive a quintet and a concerto from Wolfgang, and the viola part for the composer himself. Thus K. 498 is chamber music of the most private and intimate kind. But when Einstein remarks that, in this work, exceptionally, 'E flat major is not the key of freemasonry, but the key of intimate friendship', he would seem to be making an unreal distinction. For Mozart, true friendship was the very

Prague, the Bertramka Villa, seen from the courtyard. Mozart and Constanze stayed here during their second visit to Prague for the first performance of *Don Giovanni* in October 1787.

lifeblood of freemasonry; both Jacquin and Stadler were active fellow-freemasons, the clarinet figured prominently in music for masonic ceremonies, and in the opening *Andante*, which is both first movement and slow movement, wholly lyrical and yet a convincing sonata-type expression, contraries are reconciled in a way that was central to the masonic outlook. As Einstein himself emphasizes, Mozart's 'consciousness of his membership in the order permeates his entire [later] work'.

The *Prague* Symphony, which likewise contains masonic features, was written in Vienna in readiness for a visit to Prague occasioned by a production of *Figaro*. This otherwise large-scale Viennese symphony has no minuet, which may reflect the composer's assessment of his Prague audience. The minuet was a 'courtly' form, but in Prague the forces of the Enlightenment were known to be strong. One of the reasons for this strength is that enlightened thinking was reinforced by the long and frustrated tradition of Bohemian nationalism: in the face of the centralizing, Germanizing policies of Joseph II, to be 'radical' was to be patriotic. The feeling of national unrest in Prague was undoubtedly a factor in the overwhelming enthusiasm for *Figaro*, which Wolfgang experienced at first hand. He and Constanze arrived towards the middle of January 1787 and attended two performances, the second of which Wolfgang himself conducted. He was acclaimed like a popular hero, and everywhere he went, *Figaro* overtook him—even at a ball:

> I looked on . . . with the greatest pleasure while all these people flew about in sheer delight to the music of my *Figaro*, arranged for quadrilles and waltzes. For here they talk about nothing but *Figaro*. Nothing is played, sung, or whistled but *Figaro*. No opera is drawing like *Figaro*. Nothing, nothing but *Figaro*. Certainly a great honour for me!

The *Prague* Symphony was also received with enthusiasm. It needs to be stated plainly that, in richness, depth and symphonic power, the *Prague* is comparable with the last three symphonies—Nos. 39–41—written eighteen months later. The slow introduction is spacious and monumental beyond all precedent; the following *Allegro* is full of activity, much of it contrapuntal, and similarly in the finale imitative counterpoint plays an important part. The *Andante* combines a feline grace that is peculiarly Mozartian with many changing qualities of expression: something of the atmosphere of both *Figaro* and *Don Giovanni* may be detected here. The *Presto* finale is one of the swiftest: one of the tensest, too, due largely to a syncopated figure built into the principal theme—bars 3 and 4 (first violins). The opening bars of the

finale also show the propulsive power to be achieved by means of 'motivic counterpoint': that is, the imitative contrapuntal treatment of melodic motives—one of the crucial discoveries of the Classical style, and fundamental to this particular movement. None of Mozart's mature symphonies is closer to the world of *opera buffa*, yet none is more personal or more serious. Its zestful intensity seems to have appealed immediately to the Prague musical public.

While in Prague, Wolfgang and Constanze enjoyed the lavish hospitality of Count Johann Thun, and through him Wolfgang had introductions to many of the leading freemasons. No wonder they stayed on until mid-February, for this was one of the happiest episodes in the composer's life and certainly his greatest artistic triumph. Moreover, Pasquale Bondini, the theatre manager responsible for putting on *Figaro*, commissioned a new *opera buffa* with a fee of 100 gulden. Financially, too, the stay in Prague was a success: according to Leopold's sources, Wolfgang's earnings had amounted to no less than 1000 gulden.

Leopold was nearing the end of his life. Although in February he visited Munich, he was not at all well, and a month later was visibly failing. At the beginning of April, Nannerl wrote to Wolfgang to tell him how grave the situation had become. In a letter to Leopold dated 4 April, Wolfgang expressed views on death which are clearly masonic rather than Catholic:

Prague, the National Theatre, now the Tyll Theatre; drawing by Vincenz Marstadt, *c.* 1840. *Don Giovanni* and *La clemenza di Tito* were first performed here.

Don Giovanni, the graveyard scene in Act II; watercolour by Julius Quaglio, 1789. A design for a production at Mannheim in 1789. In the duet 'O statua gentilissima' Leporello, bolstered by Don Giovanni, invites the statue of the Commendatore to supper. The statue replies to the accompaniment of trombones, in opera-houses long associated with the supernatural.

I need hardly tell you how greatly I am longing to receive some reassuring news from yourself. And I still expect it; although I have now made a habit of being prepared in all affairs of life for the worst. As death, when we come to consider it closely, is the true goal of our existence, I have formed during the last few years such close relations with this best and truest friend of mankind, that his image is not only no longer terrifying to me, but is indeed very soothing and consoling! And I thank my God for graciously granting me the opportunity (you know what I mean) of learning that death is the *key* which unlocks the door to our true happiness. I never lie down at night without reflecting that—young as I am—I may not live to see another day. Yet no one of all my acquaintances would say that in company I am morose or disgruntled. For this blessing I daily thank my Creator and wish with all my heart that each one of my fellow-creatures could enjoy it.

Leopold was probably suffering from dropsy. After a marked

Don Giovanni, the descent into hell; from a series of eight engravings, after J. H. Ramberg, Leipzig, 1825 (see also p. 120). When the statue of the Commendatore comes to supper, the unrepentant Don is seized by demons and dragged down to hell (Act II, Finale).

improvement, which enabled Nannerl to return to St Gilgen, he died suddenly on 28 May at the age of 68. He was buried in the graveyard of the Sebastianskirche, in the Linzergasse, where many years later Constanze was placed in the same grave.

Towards the end of April, Wolfgang was himself seriously ill and was again attended by Dr Barisani, who in 1784 had recognized the symptoms of kidney disease. From now on, periods of lassitude and low vitality were to become a part of Wolfgang's life. Nonetheless, he retained an astonishing capacity for concentrated work. As well as *Don Giovanni* (K. 527), written in fulfilment of the Prague commission, the

works dating from 1787 include three string quintets—see Chapter 9—the Serenade, *Eine kleine Nachtmusik* (K. 525), *Ein musikalischer Spass* (A Musical Joke, K. 522), the Piano Sonata in C for four hands (K. 521) and the important Violin Sonata in A (K. 526), commonly considered the forerunner of Beethoven's *Kreutzer* Sonata. In April Beethoven himself, aged 16, had visited Vienna in order to study with Mozart, but after only a fortnight had returned to Bonn because his mother was gravely ill. Virtually nothing is known of the lessons that Mozart gave Beethoven, and Schenk thinks it 'highly unlikely' that the legendary prophecy, 'This boy will make a noise in the world', was ever made. The signs suggest that Mozart was almost wholly absorbed in *Don Giovanni*.

It was Da Ponte who suggested the Don Juan legend, and his reason may have been severely practical: time was short; he was already committed to produce librettos for Martín y Soler and Salieri, and a 'crib' for Don Juan had recently come to hand. The latter was *Il convitato di pietra* (The Stone Guest), a new *opera buffa* by Giovanni Bertati, a well-known librettist, and Giuseppe Gazzaniga. If Da Ponte adapted much from Bertati, he also drew from other sources, notably Goldoni and Molière, and always he effected improvements. Like *Figaro*, *Don Giovanni* is full of incident, which is a reflection of Da Ponte's dramatic sense and an important element in the lasting appeal of both operas. Moreover, Mozart found his librettist at one with his desire to tighten the construction and quicken the pace. This meant shorter arias and a still greater emphasis on dramatic conversation. In *Don Giovanni* there is only one soliloquy, for Donna Elvira, and even that is a special case, for it is overheard and commented upon by Giovanni and Leporello.

In discussing the score of *Il convitato di pietra*, Dent vividly portrays the difference between a conventional *opera buffa* of Mozart's time and one by Mozart himself:

> Gazzaniga's music is certainly dramatic, and it is also reasonable. . . . But from beginning to end there is not a single theme of any real musical significance. Every figure, vocal or instrumental, is a stock pattern, a dummy with neither life nor originality. Compared with Mozart's, it suggests a rehearsal at which the actors walk through their parts in their ordinary clothes, on an empty stage in daylight. And the music moves slowly too . . .; if it were a play, we should say that the actors are very slow at taking up their cues.

Le nozze di Figaro: Teresa Stratas as Susanna and Agnes Baltsa as Cherubino, Royal Opera House, Covent Garden, London, 1977. As she sings the aria 'Venite inginocchiatevi', Susanna disguises Cherubino as herself (Act II)—a striking example of Mozart's and Da Ponte's flair for interest on the stage.

What makes this comparison so valuable is the total absence of such a work from the modern opera-goer's experience. The nearest one is likely

to get to it is Domenico Cimarosa's masterpiece, *Il matrimonio segreto* (The Secret Marriage, libretto by Bertati), which is too distinguished to be representative.

It is not in the least surprising that *Don Giovanni* was condemned by some for its 'exaggerated, debauching contrasts'. There are aspects that are closer than *Figaro* to mainstream *opera buffa*—Leporello, for instance, is the traditional comic servant in a way that Figaro certainly is not—but there are other aspects which the Romantics, from E. T. A. Hoffmann onwards, were able to seize upon and misinterpret from their own point of view. These differences may well reflect a conscious dualism in Mozart's and Da Ponte's response to the legend: on the one hand, sympathy with Giovanni's 'heroic' defiance of convention, but on the other, condemnation of the aristocratic libertine who destroys his fellow men. To what extent there is a calculated anti-aristocratic emphasis can hardly be determined: Masetto's aria (*Hò capito*) is strong stuff—this may be said to parallel Figaro's *Se vuol bellare, signor Contino*—but was written as an afterthought, during rehearsals. Mozart's main interest seems to have been in the dramatic sweep of the whole and in achieving psychological penetration at every stage. His involvement was perhaps less complete, less unified, than in *Figaro*: for instance, it is generally agreed that Don Ottavio, though well endowed musically, is incapable of engaging an audience's sympathy.

Again the ensembles show an unprecedented flair for lyric drama, and in all those elements that some call tragic, others Romantic—most of all, the music for the Commendatore and for Don Giovanni's descent into hell—the score is strikingly prophetic. But the most fundamental development is so pervasive that it is easily taken for granted: the distinctiveness of the *Don Giovanni* sound. In the rough-and-tumble of conventional *opera buffa*, many a number, arias especially, might be freely transferred from one work to another; but from the beginning of the overture, *Don Giovanni* has a particular musical presence. In this eighteenth-century operatic world, such particularity and serious intentions are inseparable.

Wolfgang and Constanze returned to Prague at the beginning of October. Then came the usual intensive writing and rewriting and the seemingly inevitable delays: some last-minute additions have left their mark on the orderliness of the whole. The first performance, on 29 October, was another triumph, and there were three more performances within the next six days. 'Perhaps the opera will be given in Vienna after all,' remarked the composer.

PIANO CONCERTOS AND STRING QUINTETS

From the winter of 1787 to 1788 onwards, Mozart's life as a freelance in Vienna became increasingly problematical. The mixture of teaching, playing and composing had until then yielded an acceptable, if uncertain, income, but at this stage there was a marked decline which was never really overcome. The usual explanations leave much to be accounted for. These are firstly the 'fickleness' of the Viennese public—a convenient, superficial notion—secondly the intrigues of Mozart's rivals, and thirdly the kind of music that Mozart was now writing. So far as the fashionable public is concerned, there is substance in this last point. Even as good a musician as Dittersdorf, who recognized in Mozart 'one of the greatest of original geniuses', could regret that there were quite so many inspired ideas, for each one seemed to be driven out by the next and the mind became overwhelmed by an experience of superabundant beauty. What, then, did the light-minded and unmusical make of the later piano concertos, or *Don Giovanni*, or the string quintets? The ubiquitous Count Zinzendorf provides one answer. He seems to have been at everything and to have thought himself musical, but always when required to use his imagination, he reacted unfavourably.

Such resistances can be both cumulative and catching, but 'difficult' music is hardly a sufficient explanation of the apparent collapse of support for Mozart's subscription concerts. The collapse came so suddenly—more or less coincidentally with the triumphs in Prague—that one is almost bound to look for some extra-musical reason. By far the most likely is the growing suspicion of freemasonry, and particularly of its radical wing, the Illuminati, to which a number of Mozart's closest

A piano by Heilman of Mainz, *c.* 1775; a five-octave instrument typical of the pianos used by Mozart in Vienna. This particular instrument, in the Colt Clavier Collection, has been recorded—see, for example, Kenneth van Barthold's performance (1977) of Mozart's Sonata in F (K. 332), Argo ZK 43.

137

friends seem to have belonged. As early as December 1785, Joseph II had curbed the freemasons in Vienna by forcing the amalgamation of lodges and requiring that reports of activities and lists of members be submitted to the police. Quite apart from the direct effects, this was taken as a sign by all who were actively hostile to the order. In the next few years a stream of alarmist and scurrilous pamphlets did much to isolate the order, and from 1788 onwards there were political and economic tensions—for instance, bread riots in Vienna—for which the freemasons were ready scapegoats. This campaign of vilification was to culminate in the widespread belief that the order was responsible for the French Revolution.[22] In these circumstances, even Mozart's successes in 'radical' Prague may have been damaging in Vienna.

Meanwhile, the emperor continued to mete out qualified encouragement, as he had done since *Die Entführung*. When Gluck died in November 1787, Mozart was appointed to succeed him as the court 'chamber composer': a misleading term to us, for the duties consisted in providing minuets, *contredanses* and so forth for court balls! The salary of 800 gulden, though much less than Gluck had received, was customary on appointment. It has been suggested that the emperor, having heard repeated rumours of Mozart's projected departure for England, personally directed that this appointment be made. He was certainly responsible for the decision to produce *Don Giovanni* in Vienna. In the eight months from May to December 1788, the opera was given 15 times, and was then dropped completely. That it 'failed to please' is based largely on the wellnigh disastrous first night, when there was trouble with several of the singers. The subsequent performances aroused a more favourable response, though scarcely the enthusiasm that Prague had witnessed.

At this critical stage in the composer's fortunes, when much of the goodwill of previous years seems suddenly to have evaporated, it is convenient to break the narrative in order to consider the two non-vocal forms in which Mozart was most the innovator: the piano concerto and the string quintet. In broad terms, Mozart did for the piano concerto what Haydn did for the symphony; he raised it from *galant* entertainment to a serious and substantial form capable of embracing every shade of expression. As for the string quintet, with two violas, this was a major 'discovery' in 1787, and the five late masterpieces, together with the Quintet for clarinet and strings, represent the summit of Mozart's chamber music.

The solo concerto, as distinct from the *concerto grosso*, was an offspring of the operatic aria. This can be seen clearly enough in any typical *galant* concerto with its emphasis on display and its formal reliance on the

ritornello—an introductory statement by the orchestra that recurs throughout. Indeed, the *ritornello* idea survives in the orchestral 'prelude' at the beginning of the first movement in the concertos of both Mozart and Beethoven. In the *galant* concerto the relationship between soloist and orchestra—often only strings—was seldom more than a primitive alternation, and the appeal was essentially stylish and elegant. Such were the concertos that the boy Mozart had heard in Paris and London in 1764 to 1766 and had promptly imitated by adapting movements from sonatas by J. C. Bach, Raupach and others. His first original piano concerto is K. 175, in D, written in 1773, and the first important one the Concerto in E flat (K. 271) of four years later. Apart from K. 365, in E flat, for two pianos, all the subsequent piano concertos date from the Vienna period, 15 out of the 17 being concentrated in the years 1782 to 1786, the years of successful concert-giving.

Clearly, Mozart's main achievement in this form arose from his own immediate needs as a concert pianist. Equally clearly, the works themselves go far beyond what was necessary to meet those needs. Here the appropriate reference point is the successful career, likewise in Vienna, of Leopold Kozeluch. Only four years older than Mozart, Kozeluch succeeded Wagenseil in 1778 as music teacher to the imperial

The Mehlgrube in the Neuer Markt, Vienna; engraving by Johann Adam Delsenbach after Johann Bernhard Fischer von Erlach. Built in the seventeenth century for balls and other entertainments, this was the scene of many of Mozart's public concerts.

family; as a pianist he was Mozart's principal rival, and as a composer a master of well-turned pleasantries. One highly laudatory notice describes him as 'the most generally popular composer now living, and that quite rightly. His works are characterized by cheerfulness and grace, the noblest melody combined with the purest harmony and the most pleasing arrangement in respect to rhythm and modulation.' If Mozart had remained as he was, musically speaking, in 1781 to 1782, then he, too, might have received such praise; but it is precisely in the extent to which he went beyond 'cheerfulness and grace' and 'the most pleasing arrangement'—the merely predictable—that his piano concertos are great and enduring.

Once again it is a matter of serious intentions, and these are proclaimed as early as K. 271; in the wealth of ideas, the formal spaciousness and intricacy, and all the little imaginative touches which tell us at once that this is the music of Mozart. In describing the nature of his Viennese concertos, there is no need to lean on the two great works in minor keys, amazing though they are; some of the major-key concertos are equally revealing—if not more so, for they appear to start out on conventional ground. Naturally, seriousness meant bringing soloist and orchestra into a closer partnership, replacing alternation with interaction, and this in turn meant fusing soloistic bravura and symphonic development. In some of these concertos—none more so than the C minor (K. 491) and the C major (K. 503)—the symphonic urge is deep and strong; but in general the interaction of the themes more closely resembles the interplay of characters in the operas. This applies particularly to the opening movements, where the internal relationships are continually changing and nothing can be taken for granted. Whoever first called these movements 'voiceless dramas' had a clear insight into their nature and affinity. As well as operatic and symphonic elements, however, the piano concertos contain ideas that are almost chamber-musical, and there are many distinctive passages in which the wind instruments are treated as a *concertante* group in dialogue with the piano or the strings. Among the slow movements are several of Mozart's most memorable expressions in minor keys, and the finales show a seemingly limitless resourcefulness in handling the rondo principle.

Closer comment follows on some six or seven of these works, chosen for particular qualities of expression. The Concerto in F (K. 459), the last of six concertos written in 1784, may be said to exemplify many of the characteristics mentioned above. The spaciousness and subtlety of the opening movement is especially notable for the way in which the familiar dotted rhythm of its principal theme is repeatedly renewed and given fresh meaning. The slow movement foreshadows Susanna's *canzonetta* in Act III of *Figaro*, and the brilliant rondo finale combines the rhythmic zest of *opera buffa* with passages of closely wrought counterpoint. The D minor Concerto (K. 466) is the next in the series and the most overtly dramatic: the impassioned outer movements were given cadenzas by Beethoven and won the enthusiasm of the Romantics, most of whom knew very few of Mozart's concertos. The slow movement, in B flat major, is actually headed *Romanze*; but the tensions in this work, however acute and disruptive, are classically balanced and contained, enabling Hutchings to describe the finale as 'the most wonderfully organised rondo in all music'.[23] The first movement reminds us that D minor is to be the key for the stone guest in *Don Giovanni*, and yet, even here, the initial motive is one of the commonest of Mozartian commonplaces—a brisk rising triplet figure, most familiar from the opening of the *Jupiter* Symphony.

The next three concertos to be mentioned were completed while *Figaro* was in progress. The first of these, in E flat (K. 482), is sometimes slighted as a partial reversion to *galant* entertainment, as if every subsequent work ought necessarily to have the intensity of K. 466! True, the scope of the first movement is more a matter of richness of material than of elaborate tonal argument, but those who are fond of stressing Mozart's concessions to his public should note the way in which C minor is dramatically arrived at at the beginning of the development. The spirit at this point is almost Beethovenian, and the plot, so to speak, is far-reaching, C minor being the key in which the unique *Andante*, consisting of variations, but with interludes in major keys, is to be placed. The finale, based on a hunting-style tune with a number of offshoots, is wittily inventive throughout, and it is not hard to imagine the composer himself adding spontaneous embellishments. In the middle of this finale there is an *Andantino cantabile* in A flat, which features the wind band and takes us closer to *Figaro* than any other passage in the work.

The Concerto in A (K. 488) is perhaps the most purely lyrical of the mature concertos, and certainly the one that is closest to *Figaro*. There are no trumpets and drums, and, as in K. 482, clarinets replace oboes: lightness, buoyancy, warmly sensuous textures—these abound in the outer movements, which are Mozart at his happiest. Happiest, not gaiest, though there is gaiety as well: the distinction implies an underlying composure, and this, in turn, means an awareness of other states. How else could such 'simple', song-like expressions belong so naturally with the *Andante* in F sharp minor? The key might be passed off as the relative minor, which it is. Nonetheless, F sharp minor is rare in Mozart, and here it is the scene of one of the most poignant expressions of suffering to be found anywhere in his music. A truly Classical composure—a quality suggestive of Winckelmann's 'noble simplicity and calm grandeur'—is a part of that poignancy, at once heightening and mitigating the chromatic expressiveness (*Ex. 2*).

On hearing the Concerto in C minor (K. 491), Beethoven is said to have exclaimed: 'In this art, he is the master of us all.' There are several ways in which the C minor is the concerto closest to Beethoven: it is the most symphonic and most concentrated, has an almost Beethovenian aggressiveness in the finale—consider some of the piano writing, especially from bar 65 (*Ex. 3*) and similar passages—and deploys the largest orchestra. In the opening movement the orchestra is a powerful protagonist; every ounce of weight is used in the 'tuttis', and the orchestra alone has possession of the arresting first phrase of the principal theme. This twelve-bar theme, heard at the outset, touches all twelve notes and is Mozart at his most chromatic (*Ex. 4*). After a development that culminates in a succession of impassioned dominant sevenths, each 'resolving' only on the next, the recapitulation is a profound re-thinking of the earlier course of events. The serene *Larghetto* is in E flat major, but C minor still casts a shadow: see, for instance, the first of the elaborate *concertante* passages for the woodwind (*Ex. 5*). The finale is not a rondo but continuous variations on a tersely constructed, march-like theme. The phrase structure, the latent chromaticism and the interaction of minor and major are sources of sustained tension. Moreover, this finale not only begins but ends in the minor mode, the song-like (*Figaro*-like) episode in C major notwithstanding.

This most intensive period of concerto writing ended with the C major (K. 503), designed as an even larger-scale counterpart to the C minor: the avowedly majestic (*maestoso*) first movement is the largest that Mozart wrote in any form, and one of the grandest. Although a little stiff and lacking in spontaneity, K. 503 is one of those works that compel us to reflect on what Mozart might have written if he had continued developing alongside Beethoven. At the time of Beethoven's *Eroica* Symphony, Mozart would still have been under 50. The D major Concerto (*Coronation*—K. 537) of 1788 may be passed over as one of the less inventive—it seems to have been written, like the last three symphonies, for concerts that did not take place—but the B flat (K. 595) is of special interest. Written in 1791, this stands somewhat apart from the others and is characterized by that renewal of simplicity—Einstein calls it a 'second naiveté'—which distinguishes the music of Mozart's last year. In this instance it is a simplicity that masks, or reveals, much sadness: sadness disguised as 'gaiety' and 'entertainment', but subtly inflecting familiar turns of phrase, harmonic progressions and even types of movement—the *Larghetto*, for instance. Appropriately, the dancing

rondo tune in the finale (*Ex. 6a*) was used again by Mozart for a song entitled *Sehnsucht nach dem Frühlinge* (Longing for Spring, K. 596 [*Ex. 6b*]). As well as being uniquely expressive, K. 595 is remarkably varied and resourceful in its combining of piano and orchestra, and it is wonderfully scored, without clarinets, trumpets and drums.

The immediate practical purpose that prompted the piano concertos is in no way incompatible with the idea of inner necessity: ideally, the one occasions, the other motivates. In Mozart's time nearly all music was in some sense occasioned, and so it has long been supposed that the string quintets of 1787 must have been written with an end in view. But all we know is that in that year Mozart first arranged the wind Serenade in C minor (K. 388) as a string quintet (K. 406) and then wrote the C major Quintet (K. 515) and the G minor (K. 516), two of his greatest masterpieces. In the following year, in his penury, the composer marketed all three, not very successfully, on a public subscription basis. Without a shred of evidence, and leaning heavily on the opening of K. 515, which gives prominence to the cello, some have maintained that these works were intended for the cello-playing Frederick William II, King of Prussia. The possibility of a quite different kind of prompting, though one with precedents in Mozart's work, has generally been overlooked. This, too, is speculative, but hardly frivolous.

Mozart's only previous string quintet was a boyhood work (K. 174)

String Quintet in C minor (K. 406); the first page from Mozart's autograph score. An arrangement of the Serenade for wind instruments (K. 388), this is the first of the three great string quintets written in 1787.

Concerto vocale con accompagnamento strumentale by Giuseppe Zocchi (1711–67), showing a mid-eighteenth-century chamber concert.

written in response to at least one quintet by Michael Haydn. In 1786, the year before Mozart returned to the medium, Michael Haydn wrote his admirable Quintet in F. Although designed as a *divertimento*, in seven movements, this has a substantial first movement and is remarkably Mozartian in treatment, especially in some of the uses of the two violas. Bearing in mind that Mozart always respected Michael Haydn as a composer, one can easily imagine him finding this work a revelation of immense possibilities as yet unrealized. The music he proceeded to write leaves no doubt of the impact upon him of the quintet idea, wherever it may have come from; and the choice of K. 388 for a trial run, as it were, is also indicative of inner necessity, for nothing more intensely expressive was available. Moreover, the readiness to make formal innovations fully accords with a belief that the motivation came from the medium rather than from a patron. The last two quintets, in D (K. 593) and in E flat (K. 614), were written in 1790 and 1791 for a 'Hungarian amateur'— probably Johann Tost, the wealthy merchant to whom Haydn dedicated two sets of quartets.

The quintets in C major and G minor invite comparison with the symphonies in the same keys—No. 40 in G minor and No. 41 in C

(*Jupiter*)—written just one year later. Like the *Jupiter* Symphony, K. 515 is a radiant work in which the element of dramatic conflict is contained and absorbed by an overall 'harmoniousness' and sense of order. But the two works in G minor, the most passionate and melancholic of Mozart's minor keys, are fraught with harrowing, disruptive tensions that are the more heart-rending because the music is free from the self-conscious stressfulness of the *Sturm und Drang* era: 'all the "properties" of "Storm and Stress" are divested of rhetoric, so that the drama is pure music and the music drama, and the suffering is neither Mozart's nor ours, but mankind's'.[24] In other words, these are Classical works, which universalize and exhilarate.

The first movement of K. 515 is full of hidden treasure, both harmonic and contrapuntal, though this is not even hinted at in the simple opening dialogue. (Incidentally, this opening shows one of the basic capabilities of the medium: three-part harmony in the middle of the texture, with the first violin and cello entirely freed for thematic work [*Ex. 7*].) It soon transpires that here, perhaps more than in any previous work by Mozart, the exposition contains much that is of the nature of development; accordingly, the scale is large, and the 'true' development is so much the more richly composed. The very concise minuet, placed second, is drawn entirely from its opening figure; by way of contrast, the trio is unusually diverse. The big *Andante* is full of mellifluous dialogue, tender and serene, and is one of those movements in which Mozart's special feeling for the viola, his own string instrument, is decisive. The finale is a brilliant sonata-rondo, a form that Haydn made his own but Mozart seldom used.

Magnificent though K. 515 is, its successor, the G minor, is even more remarkable. This is perhaps the most deeply pathetic work in the chamber music repertory. If it were possible to reduce the ripeness of Mozart's imagination to a handful of general principles, the following would doubtless emerge as pathetic agents: the use of chromatically falling melody, especially in the opening *Allegro*; the interaction of minor and major keys, the latter serving to heighten rather than relieve the sense of sadness; the prevalence of imitative counterpoint, often in a kind of echoing dialogue, and the use of silence, in all or all but one of the parts, especially in the first and third movements. None of these should be separated from the wonderfully telling harmonic progressions.

For two movements, G minor is well-nigh absolute. In the opening movement, even the *second* subject (*Ex. 9*) begins in that key, and with a melodic emphasis on the minor third (B flat); only gradually is the expected key (B flat major) arrived at. This music is sustained, however, by a rhythmic current of repeated quavers, as in the first movement of

Ex. 6   K. 595

a) Allegro

K. 596

b)

Komm, lie-ber Mai, und ma — che die Baü- me wie – der grün
(Come, love-ly May, and make ——— the bran-ches green   a – gain)

Ex. 7   K. 515

Ex. 8 Adagio   K. 593

Ex. 9   K. 516

Ex. 10   Allegro   Trio   K. 516

Ex. 11   K. 516

K. 515, and so it sings and dances in the Classical manner, no matter how intense the emotional content. The minuet is again placed second and is perhaps Mozart's most astonishing creation in this form. The form, as such, is intact, but the content is wholly personal, in the second part of the trio amounting to a glorious little instrumental madrigal. This trio is in G major and depends entirely on a 'translation' into the major of the cadence-figure at the end of the minuet (*Ex. 10*). There is a similar transformation in the slow movement (*Ex. 11*) where the darkness of the contrasting theme (from bar 18) is made more telling by its translation into light—an innocent, dance-like passage in the major (from bar 27). This muted *Adagio*—not a common marking in Mozart—is another creation of the first importance, beginning with breadth and serenity, but soon becoming an expression of profound loneliness. Against the prevailing G minor, its key of E flat major is treated as a region of longing. The finale is a large-scale rondo in G major, preceded by a slow introduction in the minor that might almost be described as Romantic, so intense and insistent is its harrowing expressiveness. Mozart probably saw this second *Adagio* as a purging of the darker emotions and a

A satirical drawing by Hogarth produced for a concert ticket. Compare this with the Zocchi (page 145) where the players are grouped in orderly fashion around the harpsichord, from which the performance is directed; in contrast, here, all is in disarray.

transition to light—or even to Light, in the masonic sense—but to the more Romantically inclined it is capable of making the bright, buoyant rondo as hard to accept as the 'comic' ending to *Don Giovanni*. Not that there is any suggestion of *opera buffa* in this finale; it is simply an athletic, major-key piece in 6/8 time, without any real shadows, thereby discharging the Classical function of such a finale, which is to resolve tension.

In the last two quintets, as in other late works, there is a strong tendency for the element of dramatic conflict, rooted in the sonata principle, to be transformed by 'harmonious' counterpoint and by thematic cross-references between subjects. For example, in the opening movement of the D major Quintet, although there is great thematic tension and variety, there is little of the expected opposition of subjects, and in the E flat major the purging of sonata dualism results in an almost monothematic first movement. A contrapuntal, even fugal, inclination is characteristic of both finales—that of the E flat is in spirit positively Haydnish—and in the two minuets there is something of that 'second naïveté' mentioned earlier in this chapter. For an insight into that, however, one can hardly do better than turn to the slow movement of the E flat, where a blissful simplicity is expressed in a fusion of rondo and variation forms. Both in poignancy and key structure, the slow movement (*Adagio*) of the D major (*Ex. 8*) is comparable with that of the G minor. The initial idea, with its contrasting effects of full and open textures, makes wonderful use of the two violas: notice especially the richness achieved in the part-writing of the first two bars (and their equivalents) and the almost antiphonal treatment of the broken, fluttering descent (bars 9–12). The answering section, in the minor, is a dialogue between first violin and cello, with dark, pulsating harmonies in the inner parts: music that points towards the chamber works of Schubert rather than of Beethoven. Here again the second viola is indispensable to the texture.

In listening closely to these string quintets, it will become clear that all the points mentioned above concern Mozart's imagination and the listener's experience; they are not 'technicalities' of interest only to musicians. Many insights can be gained, of which the most rewarding are not accessible in any other way.

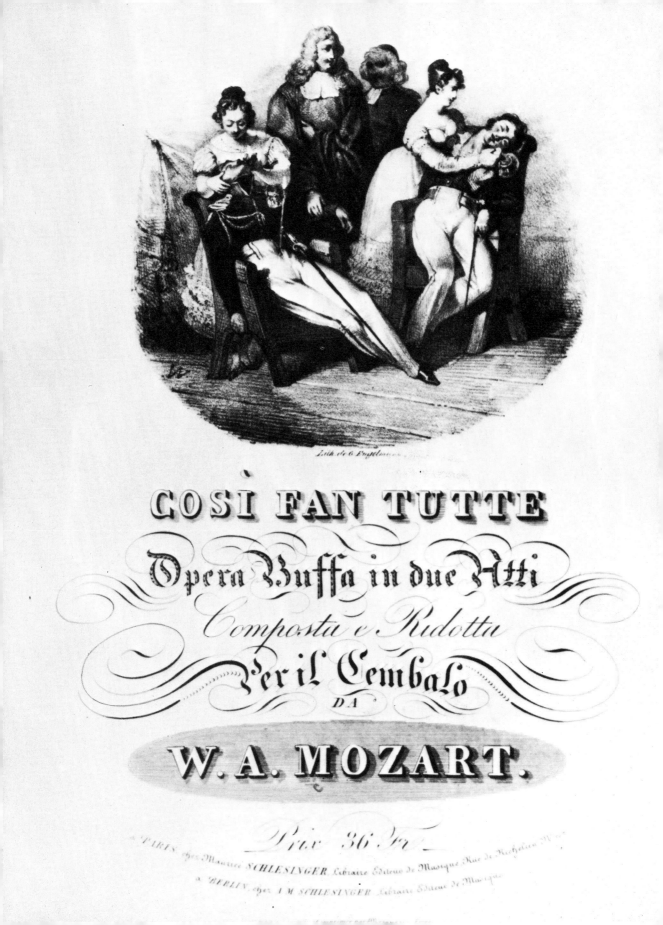

POVERTY AND RICHES

During the year 1788 Mozart's situation, both publicly and privately, became critical. The apparent collapse of his concert public has already been touched on. The subscription concerts attempted in June were a failure, and subsequent promotions seem to have fared no better. In the summer of 1789 a subscription list for some concerts to be given at Mozart's house came back with only one name on it. Of the many high-ranking, influential supporters of former years, it would seem that Baron van Swieten alone remained loyal. Swieten's private concerts became the only opportunities for such music-making but were generally unremunerative. True, *Don Giovanni* ran for 15 performances, and in 1789 *Figaro* was successfully revived. For us, these operatic events complicate the question of 'fickleness' and 'fashion', underlining the need for caution; for Mozart, their reward can only have been artistic. There were no performing rights; a composer received a fee for writing an opera, but in general, apart from the proceeds of benefit performances, he stood to gain little more. The main longer-term reward of a successful opera was in having others commissioned.

Financially, Mozart was driven to makeshift expedients which he hoped would bridge the gap between present misfortune and future success. The first real crisis was in June 1788, when the landlord demanded an immediate payment of arrears. This resulted in a panicky move to cheap accommodation in the suburb of Wahring and, simultaneously, one of the earliest letters to Michael Puchberg asking for money. The request was for assistance 'for a year or two with one or two thousand *gulden*, at a suitable rate of interest':

Così fan tutte, title-page of piano score with lithograph by G. Engelmann, published by Schlesinger, Paris, 1822. The first piano score of *Così* was published in 1795, the first full score in 1810. This is Mozart's last *opera buffa*, and the libretto is Da Ponte's masterpiece.

If you should find it inconvenient to part with so large a sum at once, then I beg you to lend me until to-morrow at least a couple of hundred *gulden*, as my landlord in the Landstrasse has been so importunate that in order to avoid an unpleasant incident I have had to pay him on the spot, and this has made things very awkward for me! We are sleeping to-night, for the first time, in our new quarters, where we shall remain both summer and winter. On the whole the change is all the same to me, in fact I prefer it. As it is, I have very little to do in town, and as I am not exposed to so many visitors, I shall have more time for work. If I have to go to town on business, which will certainly not be very often, any *fiacre* will take me there for ten *kreutzer*. Moreover our rooms are cheaper and during the spring, summer and autumn more pleasant. . . .

Perhaps the most disturbing statement is 'very little to do in town'. There is an air of withdrawal from Vienna and its musical life. At the time, however, Mozart did not have any commissions from elsewhere, so it is hard to see how his situation could have improved. Inevitably, appeals to Puchberg, and to others, were renewed frequently, usually with a reference to money that could not fail to be received shortly: some outstanding payment from abroad, the salary paid quarterly by the court, or subscription fees. The most moving aspect of these letters is the gradual change in tone, from one of dignity and apparent self-confidence to one that is pleading, desperate and demoralized. Inseparable from this change in tone is a loss of credibility; with each renewal of indebtedness, the prospect of repayment became more remote, the begging more painfully obvious. Exactly how much was borrowed during the three and a half years from June 1788 it is impossible to say, but at the time of his death, Mozart's debts amounted to some 3000 gulden. The only cause for surprise is that the sum was not appreciably larger.

Michael Puchberg was a wealthy friend who had inherited the textile manufacturing business in which he had been an employee. It is likely that Mozart had first met him many years before, but a close friendship developed only when they came to know each other as fellow freemasons. Puchberg did not take up the suggestion of a loan of 'one or two thousand *gulden*'—it may be deduced from the letter quoted above that Mozart did not really expect otherwise—but he did send money to help meet immediate needs; indeed, he did so repeatedly, though usually it was a rather smaller sum than had been asked for, and sometimes he did not respond at once. Precious little, if any, of this money can have been repaid, but Puchberg received a number of compositions from Mozart,

Così fan tutte; Paolo Montarsolo as Don Alfonso (centre) with Jerry Jennings and Knut Skram as Ferrando and Guglielmo, Glyndebourne, Sussex, 1971. The two young officers accept Don Alfonso's wager that their fiancées, Dorabella and Fiordiligi, will prove unfaithful (Act I, Scene 1).

including the gracious and eloquent Piano Trio in E major (K. 542). After Mozart's death, he continued to help Constanze.

It was in the weeks immediately following the move out to Wahring that the last three symphonies were written. In the catalogue of his works which Mozart had been keeping since February 1784, the Symphony No. 39 in E flat major (K. 543) is dated 26 June, No. 40 in G minor (K. 550) 25 July, and No. 41 in C major (*Jupiter*—K. 551) 10 August. These are completion dates, and so the widespread assertion that all three symphonies were written 'within six weeks' shows excessive zeal: about two months would be more realistic. In the circumstances, the fact that they were written at all is remarkable enough. There is no evidence that any of them was played in Mozart's lifetime, but the later addition of clarinet parts to the G minor is a tantalizing pointer. However, reason insists that these symphonies must have been written with some immediate purpose in view, the most favoured suggestion being subscription concerts which failed to materialize. (One fact should make us pause: never before had Mozart written symphonies expressly for Vienna.) Whatever the truth may be, at another level this extraordinary creative outpouring, matched, if at all, only in 1786, was a superb gesture of defiance, for the composer must have known that there was little in these works to appeal to the Zinzendorfs—and much, especially in the G minor, that such listeners would find distasteful.

There are no known symphonies of an earlier date on so grand a scale. However, it is not the scale, as such, but the richness of content that gives these works their importance: a richness accommodated by familiar designs, with few of the formal surprises associated with Haydn. No. 40 (G minor) is arguably the greatest symphony before Beethoven, and the *Jupiter* is the first true 'finale-symphony'.

No. 39 has been described as 'Mozart's farewell to his youth'; but this remark seems to have been prompted by qualities common to a long succession of works in E flat major—Mozart's masonic key. According to Einstein, Katharine Thomson and others, No. 39 is very much a masonic composition, not only luminous in spirit but also rich in symbolism. This may well have a bearing on the triple measure (3/4) of the first *Allegro*, of which the principal theme uses (masonic?) tied notes and an aspiring major sixth (*Ex. 12*).[25] (Classical first movements in triple time are rare indeed: apart from that of Beethoven's *Eroica* Symphony, also in E flat, what others come to mind?) The shape of the theme is unusual, as is its complete absence from the development section. The *Andante* is of an almost unprecedented gravity and depth, and its closing theme (from bar 53) is an excellent example of the serious polyphonic writing for woodwind characteristic of Mozart's last years. The manner

Five-keyed B flat clarinet, made of boxwood by Mousseter, Paris, *c.* 1780. Mozart's trio, quintet and concerto are the earliest classics for the clarinet, but it was at Mannheim that the instrument was first popularized.

of the minuet is ceremonial, but with a popular vigour. This popular strain is unmistakable in the trio, which features the two clarinets, the one playing the tune, the other providing a 'chobbling' accompaniment. The athletic finale is one of Mozart's finest, and also one of his supreme expressions of optimism. Moreover, it is as if the composer had deliberately set out to beat Haydn at his own monothematic game, complete with cheeky shifts of key. The initial theme (*Ex. 13*), in whole or in part, is ubiquitous; it furnishes both subjects (sonata form), dominates the entire development, and finally clinches the coda.

Nowhere, not even in the later piano concertos and the string quintets, is Mozart's instrumental genius more powerfully affirmed than in the G minor Symphony. Not surprisingly, this is Mozart at his most independent, his furthest removed from Haydn: originality, intensity, oneness—these qualities have impressed themselves on every generation. But the nature of the impression has varied greatly, from 'Grecian lightness and grace' (Schumann) to the 'demonic'. Such extremes may seem irreconcilable, yet each contains an important part-truth. The G minor is certainly an expression of tense, anguished emotion, but it is also a structure of Classical poise and lucidity. 'Passions,' wrote Mozart, 'whether violent or not, should never be expressed when they reach an unpleasant stage; and music, even in the most terrible situations, should never offend the ear, but should charm it and always remain music.' From an eighteenth-century point of view, there are moments in the G minor Symphony, as in the piano concertos in minor keys, that stretch this artistic credo to its limits and even beyond. As already shown, Mozart was widely regarded as an extravagant, over-emotional composer. To those who found him so, Classicism was surely synonymous with convention and formality; to Mozart himself, at least in his minor-key works, it meant transmuting human pain into aesthetic pleasure, imposing his infallible sense of form on the chaos of experience—or, to adapt A. E. Housman's splendid phrase, seeking to harmonize the sorrows of the world.

Of the world, be it noted, not merely his own private sorrows. To try to interpret the G minor Symphony by reference to the composer's misfortunes in the summer of 1788 is to launch out in quite the wrong direction. The Classical artist universalizes; he draws on the richness of his own experience, but what he achieves is an objective statement—in this case 'about' suffering—not an expression of his own condition. Three of the four movements (1, 3 and 4) are in G minor: such an insistence on the minor mode, especially in the finale, is most unusual in a Classical symphony. It follows that the basic conception is by no means identical with that of the string quintet in the same key; even the two

slow movements, though both in E flat major, are quite different in feeling. The acute tensions of the finale are sustained throughout—notice especially the rugged motivic counterpoint in the development (*Ex. 14*)—and this imparts an air of protest and defiance far removed from the brightness and buoyancy of the (major-key) finale of the quintet.[26]

The title of No. 41 in C is not Mozart's, but as well as being useful for reference—the sole justification of most such titles—*Jupiter* directs our thoughts to the only movement that could have prompted it, the finale. It is no extravagance to describe this finale as one of the marvels of Classical music: a superbly wrought sonata form, saturated with imitative counterpoint and carried off with an incomparable lightness and ease. It is often stated that there are five themes or motives (*Ex. 15*); four is more realistic, the so-called fifth being distinguished from the third only by a prefix of four notes (oboe, bar 76). None of these ideas is remarkable in itself, and the first (C–D–F–E) is nothing other than an old Baroque tag. The Idea transcends the ideas, the overall conception the material that defines it: consider the great coda in which all four or five motives are worked together in fugal style and the Idea emerges in its most concentrated form. The controlled ecstasy of this coda is splendidly highlighted by the tense, chunky-textured development section where the Idea is threatened with fragmentation. Such long-term connections come naturally and inevitably in a movement as unified as this one.

The opening movement, too, uses simple materials. Those of the first subject are entirely stock-in-trade: a well-worn call to attention, a familiar little sequence and some commonplace cadence-making chords—and yet the effect is fresh and spontaneous. The second subject (strings alone [*Ex. 16*]) is all elegance and grace, the sort of writing that Richard Strauss must have had in mind when he said that Mozart's melody 'hovers like Plato's Eros between heaven and earth, between mortality and immortality—set free from "the will" '.[27] One of the 'secrets' of its sound is the space between the singing first violins and the accompanying seconds. The thrusting contrapuntal passage in the development (*Ex. 17*) takes as its starting-point (*x*) a simple little cadence-figure in the *opera buffa* tune that is the closing theme: literally an *opera buffa* tune, for it was written by Mozart for an additional aria—*Un bacio di mano* (K. 541)—in an opera by Anfossi. The *Andante* is a model of Mozartian refinement, truly *cantabile*, but with a climax that is Beethovenian and a 'bridge' (from bar 18) that seems almost to have strayed from the slow movement of the G minor, so absorbed, even visionary, is its feeling. The minuet grows entirely from its first, chromatically descending phrase, and the trio juxtaposes naïveté and self-awareness—an anticipation of the finale's basic motive (C–D–E–F)—in a way that is dramatic and in the context extraordinary.

The autumn and winter of 1788 brought no encouragement. So little appears to have been happening that, for the first time, one begins to wonder how Mozart spent his days. Was he taking pupils again, and if so, to what extent? This is not at all clear, but we know that Puchberg, on at least one occasion, suggested teaching as a stop-gap. Meanwhile, living

Ex. 15

Ex. 16

Ex. 17

out at Wahring was proving impracticable. Whether it was the need for pupils, or Swieten's concerts, or simply the rigours of winter, we cannot tell, but something brought the Mozarts back into town. After the death of Joseph Starzer in 1787, Mozart had taken over the direction of Swieten's oratorio concerts. Earlier in 1788, he had given performances of C. P. E. Bach's *Die Auferstehung und Himmelfahrt Jesu* (The Resurrection and Ascension of Jesus), and he now prepared new instrumental parts for Handel's *Acis and Galatea*. He subsequently did likewise for *Messiah* and other works by Handel, a composer Swieten was actively reviving.

Johann Wilhelm Hässler; engraving, by C. Müller. This Dresden musician was a celebrated organist and pianist. Mozart competed with him and was not impressed: 'his playing is not thorough . . . he is far from being an Albrechtsberger'.

In the spring of 1789, Mozart jumped at the chance to accompany Prince Lichnowsky, a fellow freemason and former pupil, on a visit to Berlin. It was partly the old urge to travel, partly a belief in something better beyond the horizon, but perhaps most of all a desire to escape from the sheer depression of remaining in Vienna. There was justification in the fact that Frederick William II was genuinely musical and prepared to pay up, but the departure was hasty and quite unplanned. At the Prussian court, however, there was an ally in Mozart's old friend Ramm, the oboist, who was able to prepare the ground.

The journey northwards was by way of Prague, where friends were visited, Dresden and Leipzig. At Dresden, Mozart played before the Elector Frederick Augustus III and engaged in a contest with Johann Hässler, a celebrated pianist and organist whom he afterwards declared to be 'incapable of executing a fugue properly'. Vitality and bravado come through strongly in his letters to Constanze, but so does his longing to be reunited with her:

> Dearest little wife, if only I had a letter from you! If I were to tell you all the things I do with your dear portrait, I think that you would often laugh. For instance, when I take it out of its case, I say, 'Good-day, Stanzerl!—Good-day, little rascal, pussy-pussy, little turned-up nose, little bagatelle, *Schluck und Druck*', and when I put it away again, I let it slip in very slowly, saying all the time, 'Nu—Nu—Nu—Nu!' with the peculiar emphasis which this word so full of meaning demands, and then just at last, quickly, 'Good night, little mouse, sleep well.' Well, I suppose I have been writing something very foolish (to the world at all events); but to us who love each other so dearly, it is not foolish at all. To-day [13 April] is the sixth day since I left you and by Heaven! it seems a year.

The letters to Constanze reveal a warm, close, playful relationship; he is still Pedrillo to her Blonde. . . . But there is also an underlying anxiety; he asks for 'more details' of what she is doing, begs her 'not to go out walking alone—and preferably not to go out walking at all', and urges her 'not only to be careful of your honour and mine, but also to consider appearances'. A few months later, when Constanze was taking the 'cure' at Baden, this same concern about her decorum was renewed. One possible explanation is that Mozart was too aware of his own susceptibility not to be anxious.

At Leipzig a visit to the Thomaskirche, where J. S. Bach's immediate successor, Johann Doles, was still cantor, resulted in Mozart giving an informal public recital on Bach's organ. He was much impressed with a Bach motet sung for him by the choir and took away with him copies of several motets. A concert given in the Gewandhaus must have reminded him of some of his best experiences at Prague, Vienna and elsewhere, for after playing the Concertos K. 456 and 503 and accompanying a friend from Prague—the soprano Josepha Dušek, for whom he had written the intense *scena, Bella mia fiamma* (K. 528)—Mozart went on to improvise for as long as the small, but enthusiastic, audience wished. The earnings, however, were disappointing.

Potsdam and Berlin yielded a number of unexpected pleasures, including a performance of *Die Entführung* in the composer's honour and a concert given by the 11-year-old Johann Nepomuk Hummel, who had studied with Mozart in Vienna and was now on a grand tour with his father. King Frederick William II proved as good as his reputation. The story that Mozart, in deference to the emperor, declined the offer of an appointment is fairly clearly a Viennese myth, but the king commissioned a set of six string quartets, and six easy piano sonatas for the Princess Frederike, and demonstrated amply that he was no skinflint. Nonetheless, by the time that Mozart returned to Vienna (4 June), the profit from the journey was meagre; in little more than a month he was appealing to Puchberg again, and with a new urgency.

By then, the first of the Prussian quartets (K. 575) and the first sonata (K. 576) had been written, but suddenly work was made impossible by illness and worry. The letter to Puchberg (12 July) refers to 'my unfortunate illness', 'my wretched condition' and 'my poor sick wife'. Constanze, in her fifth pregnancy, was very unwell and had been prescribed the 'cure' at Baden, a fashionable spa to the south of Vienna. As soon as money was available, to Baden she went. The sociable indolence of the life there seems to have been to Constanze's liking; further visits were to follow, and so far as money is concerned, Baden may be reckoned the culminating disaster.

With the revival of *Figaro*, in August, Mozart found his vitality renewed, and in September he wrote one of his most valued chamber works, the Clarinet Quintet (K. 581). Throughout the autumn and early winter he was busy with *Così fan tutte* (freely, Women Are Like That, K. 588), his last collaboration with Da Ponte and his last *opera buffa*. This was an imperial commission, and there is a tradition that the emperor himself suggested the subject, which is said to have been prompted by a recent scandal in Vienna.

As an artificial comedy, *Così* stands much closer to the mainstream of *opera buffa* than either *Figaro* or *Don Giovanni*; at the same time, this depiction of volatile emotions shows us Mozart's and Da Ponte's realism at its sharpest and most uncomfortable. To the Romantics, who liked to think that Mozart was an unwilling participant, the spectacle of two young ladies transferring their undying devotion, within a day, from their departed fiancés to two exciting Albanians was quite unacceptable. Even now, the disturbing core of truth that it contains makes some

Leipzig, the famous Thomaskirche where J. S. Bach was cantor from 1723 until 1750. Through Swieten's enthusiasm Mozart had become deeply aware of Bach's music, and when he visited Leipzig in 1789 he delighted in improvising on Bach's organ. According to an eyewitness, he 'played with consummate artistry before a large gathering for about an hour'.

163

regard *Così* as a mere frivolity, delightful but not to be taken seriously; for Mozart, however, it was a natural extension of one important aspect of *Don Giovanni*—the study of human frailty, especially in its feminine form. The score is distinguished by a wistful warmth and purity, a veiled sadness that masquerades as gaiety: qualities already touched on in reference to the B flat Piano Concerto (K. 595), which is related to *Così* much as the concertos in E flat and A (K. 482 and 488) are to *Figaro*. As for Da Ponte's contribution, a more shapely and closely knit libretto would be hard to name.

First given on 26 January 1790, *Così* was notably successful; even Count Zinzendorf found it 'charming' and 'amusing'. But one month later Joseph II died, the theatres were closed and a scramble to win the favour of his successor, Leopold II, at once began. Rumour had it that Leopold was hostile to Salieri, and accordingly Mozart's hopes were high. He may even have seen himself appointed in Salieri's place; certainly he petitioned for the post of second *Kapellmeister*—he stressed his experience as a composer of church music, and Salieri's lack of it—

Above: Così fan tutte; Pilar Lorengar as Fiordiligi, Yvonne Minton as Dorabella, and Edith Mathis as Despina, Royal Opera House, Covent Garden, London, 1972. Despina, disguised as a doctor, revives the two 'Albanians' with a powerful magnet (Act I, Finale)—a satire on the scientific ideas of the fashionable Dr Mesmer.

Left: Mozart at a performance of *Die Entführung aus dem Serail* given in his honour at the National Theatre, Berlin, 1789. He became so involved that, during Pedrillo's aria, 'Frisch zum Kampfe' (Act II), a persistent D sharp instead of D in the second violin part brought from him the outburst, 'Damn it all, will you play D!'

and also for 'the privilege of having the musical instruction of the royal family' assigned to him. It is likely that he acted impulsively, without due preparation, and equally likely that the petition was ignored. In September, when King Ferdinand of Naples visited Vienna, an opera by Salieri and another by his pupil Joseph Weigl were duly played; Mozart was not invited to contribute in any way.

That summer Constanze was unwell again and went to Baden. Inevitably, there were repeated appeals to Puchberg, and from these we learn that Mozart himself was far from well: rheumatic pains, toothache, sleeplessness, headaches—a list suggesting low vitality and a high degree of stress. But perhaps he had reached the point at which, even with Puchberg, it seemed necessary to present himself as an object of pity. However that may be, during May and June two more Prussian quartets (K. 589 and 590) were written, and at about the same time some jottings were made for more of the piano sonatas. Ill-health and anxiety then prevailed. Despite the certainty that Frederick William II would pay well, none of the remaining three quartets and five sonatas was ever written. From October onwards there was hardly time, but the failure to complete the Prussian commission during the summer months is a clear indication of disarray, be it physical, nervous, or both.

The three completed quartets were sold to a publisher 'for a mere song, so as to get my hands on some ready money'. These are different in conception from the quartets dedicated to Haydn—see Chapter 7—and for an obvious reason. The cello-playing king wished to shine, and if one part was to be liberated soloistically, then so must the others be. In the finale of the Quartet in D (K. 575), the first to be written, this problem is solved to splendid effect, but not every movement is so convincing. The possibility that Mozart grew tired of this 'unnatural' way of writing quartets cannot be ruled out, but as an explanation of his breaking off it will hardly stand.

In October, Leopold II was to be crowned Holy Roman Emperor at Frankfurt am Main. The musical arrangements included sending a party of court musicians headed by Salieri, but there was no suggestion that Mozart should go. Why not go on his own account? The idea was irresistible; more than that, it engendered a sense of well-being and vitality. Frankfurt would be crowded with potential employers. There he would be welcomed and rewarded. Having pawned his silver to buy a coach, Mozart set off with the violinist Franz Hofer, who was the husband of Constanze's eldest sister. This proved to be his last journey westward, and it induced an unsurpassed sense of euphoria. If Leopold Mozart could have seen the letter written to Constanze on arrival at Frankfurt, he would surely have turned in his grave, for there is no more

pathetic example of his son's 'illusory visions':

> I am firmly resolved to make as much money as I can here and then return to you with great joy. What a glorious life we shall have then! I will work—work so hard—that no unforeseen accidents shall ever reduce us to such desperate straits again. . . .

The hard reality of Frankfurt, and of Mainz on the return journey, was the old familiar one: artistic success and financial failure. At Munich, where King Ferdinand of Naples was being entertained, Mozart was invited to give a concert at court. That was at least a help to his flagging morale.

The coronation of Leopold II as Holy Roman Emperor in Frankfurt Cathedral, 9 October 1790. On this occasion, as on others, Mozart's hopes of making money and finding new patrons came to nothing.

THE
LAST TWELVE
MONTHS

When Mozart returned to Vienna in November 1790, he found a letter inviting him to London. This was from one O'Reilly, who was promoting Italian opera, and the invitation was for six months—January to June 1791—during which time Mozart should write 'at least two serious or comic operas' for a fee of £300. In December there was an offer for the future from the London impresario Johann Salomon, who was about to escort Haydn on his first visit to England. Why O'Reilly's proposition was not taken up we do not know; perhaps Mozart was already committed to Schikaneder for *Die Zauberflöte*. London, however, would seem by far the best prospect that had opened before him and might well have proved the ultimate solution. It requires only a little effort to see Mozart resident in London as the illustrious successor to J. C. Bach.

The winter was active but penurious. In December the String Quintet in D was written, to be followed closely by the first of three works for a mechanical organ—commissioned by the mountebank Count Joseph Deym for his waxworks museum—and then by the Piano Concerto in B flat (K. 595). In January there was dance music to be written for the court—minuets, *contredanses*, *Ländler*—and a small group of songs for a bookseller and fellow freemason. The year that had begun was not only Mozart's last but also one of his busiest, for in it he produced two operas, the E flat String Quintet, the Clarinet Concerto and the Requiem, to mention only the major works. It is possible that the need to drive himself to the limit, especially with *La clemenza di Tito* and the Requiem, may have hastened his death, but if, as seems most likely, he was stricken

Mozart at the piano; unfinished oil painting by Josef Lange, Vienna, 1782–3. This may have been a sketch for the portrait, now lost, sent by Mozart to his father in 1783.

with uraemia, then it is a matter of months, not years, that is in question.

Emanuel Schikaneder had returned to Vienna in 1789 to take over the management of the Freihaus Theatre in the suburb of Wieden. His earlier friendship with Mozart was soon renewed, and in 1790 and 1791 the two were a good deal in each other's company, especially when Constanze was at Baden. Described by Blom as a 'shrewd man of the theatre, half artist, half charlatan', Schikaneder was the sort of friend, not to say 'boon companion', by whom Mozart could easily be exploited and perhaps led astray. He appealed to the carnival spirit, which in Mozart was never far beneath the surface, and he was also a freemason. His licence at the Freihaus Theatre was exclusively for German productions, and his speciality was popular entertainments in which farce, sentimental comedy, music and theatrical effects all had their part. It was as such an entertainment, with magic as a further attraction, that *Die Zauberflöte* began, pieced together by Schikaneder himself from the work of Wieland, Gebler and other writers. The story that Mozart was reluctant to be involved because he had never before written a magic opera is almost certainly untrue. It is far more likely that he was quick to welcome the immensely varied opportunities for music that the text presented. Besides, this fantastic fairy tale was at bottom a masonic allegory, a play of commitment to those social ideals which formed the core of Mozart's humanitarian faith.

Since 1782 or 1783 Mozart had been writing works that were overtly masonic. Among the most revealing are the unfinished cantata *Dir, Seele des Weltalls* (To Thee, Mind of the Universe, K. 429), the cantata *Die Maurerfreude* (Mason's Joy, K. 471), written in honour of the most eminent Viennese freemason, Ignaz von Born, and the *Maurerische Trauermusik* (Masonic Funeral Music, K. 477). From these it is clear that the composer associated certain musical characteristics with masonic ideas: tied notes and suspensions, descending pairs of slurred notes, parallel thirds and sixths, the rising interval of a major sixth, dotted rhythms, various rhythmic embodiments of masonic knocking rituals— these, and no doubt others too, were used consciously as musical symbols. Moreover, both complex polyphonic textures and the simplest homophony acquired masonic significance, as did the timbre of clarinets, basset horns and bassoons, especially in their lower registers. That these same characteristics are to be found in symphonies, concertos and string quartets goes without saying. What cannot be determined is the extent to which masonic symbolism was consciously and meaningfully embodied in such works. But perhaps this is an unreal question, for Mozart's involvement with masonic thought was so whole-hearted that it could hardly fail to be reflected in all his more serious creation. This becomes

Karl and Wolfgang Mozart; oil painting by Hans Hansen, *c.*1798. They were Mozart's two surviving children, Karl aged 13½ and Wolfgang 6½. Karl, though musically gifted, became a civil servant; Wolfgang studied with Hummel and Salieri and in 1804 began a musical career as pianist, teacher and composer.

170

increasingly evident in the music of his last years: the Symphonies Nos. 39 and 41, the Clarinet Quintet, the Clarinet Concerto, the Requiem, even *La clemenza di Tito*, all have indisputable masonic aspects. But *Die Zauberflöte* is wholly masonic, which means that it is quite unlike any of Mozart's previous operas. And it was written for a different public.

The Freihaus (free house: a property exempt from tax and quartering) was a huge collection of tenements built around six courtyards, in one of which a 'barn theatre' had been erected in 1786.[28] This was very much downtown and the audiences were markedly plebeian, though it is certain that *Die Zauberflöte* was seen by a wide cross-section of society. These circumstances are worth stressing, for they constitute one of several ways in which Mozart's last German opera broke new ground. Musically, it ranges from the popular songs for Papageno to the passionate coloratura of the Queen of the Night, and there is repeatedly a sense of renewal, quite apart from specifically new elements. There is ensemble and choral writing like no other, and for Sarastro and his priests 'a new sound to opera, far removed from churchliness: it might be called a kind of secular awe' (Einstein). Those who believe that Mozart died when his work was complete—even at 35—can never have listened to *Die Zauberflöte*, for it has many windows on to a new creative world.

Much of the music was written during the spring and early summer, either at home, or at Baden, where Constanze was again taking the waters, or in a wooden summer-house provided by Schikaneder in one of the Freihaus courtyards. (This famous relic now stands in the garden of the Mozarteum music academy, Salzburg.) Frequently in low spirits, a prey to anxiety and probably to uraemic depression, Mozart was much dependent on Schikaneder's good cheer and Puchberg's money. Visits to Constanze were also important: during one he wrote the exquisite little motet *Ave verum* (K. 618), which is an isolated piece of church music imbued with masonic feeling. This was for Anton Stoll, the choirmaster at Baden, who had become a friend. About a month before (early May), Mozart had written to the municipal council of Vienna offering his services as 'unpaid assistant' to Leopold Hofmann, the distinguished but sick and ageing *Kapellmeister* at St Stephen's Cathedral. This was one more bid for a permanent post, but it may in part have been motivated by thoughts of establishing a masonic style in church music, thoughts that must surely have arisen during the writing of *Die Zauberflöte*. *Ave verum* and the simple, hymn-like setting of *Hostias* in the Requiem provide brief glimpses of what that style might have been. Mozart's offer was accepted, and there were hints of a future appointment, but in the event Hofmann outlived his would-be successor.

Die Zauberflöte; Metropolitan Opera House, New York, 1966. The principal singers depicted are Adriana Maliponte as Pamina, Stuart Burrows as Tamino, and John Macurdy as Sarastro; sets and costumes by Marc Chagall.

In Patulo tibi, MAFON, adest ænigma paratum:
Rem Voce aut Signis O! mihi pande precor.
Nomine qui non es MAFON, Genio tamen idem
Esser MAFON eris, scribe vel ipse mihi.

Invenit Næpharalon n
Acuuthsuaruut 1087.

Pinxit Agatus Ræhmel Viennæ
Sculpsit Joh. Georg Klinger Norib.

XLV.

It was in July that the Requiem (K. 626) was commissioned. The facts concerning this much romanticized episode are plain enough. Count Franz Walsegg, an aristocratic amateur, wished to pass off as his own a Requiem supposedly written in memory of his wife, who had died earlier that year. There was nothing remarkable in such a deception, only Walsegg was particularly anxious that the composer should not discover his identity; hence the 'mysterious stranger' who brought the commission and who at once became the subject of wild imaginings, not least in the mind of Mozart himself. That he became obsessed with the notion that this stranger—in fact, Anton Leitgeb, son of the Mayor of Vienna—was the agent of a divine providence and had set him to compose his own Requiem shows how ill Mozart was in the summer of 1791. In September he wrote to Da Ponte that he was about to die and referred to the Requiem as his swan-song.

Also in July came the commission for *La clemenza di Tito* (The Clemency of Titus, K. 621). *Die Zauberflöte* was not quite finished, the Requiem barely begun, but for the time being everything had to be sacrificed to this coronation *opera seria* for Prague, where Leopold II was to be crowned King of Bohemia on 6 September. The coronation was a sop to Bohemian nationalism, and it was the Bohemian Estates (assembly) that decided on the libretto and the composer for it.

Above: Freihaus complex in the Wieden suburb of Vienna; engraving by Johann Ziegler, 1780. This huge collection of tenements built around six courtyards has an important place in Viennese working-class history. The theatre erected in one of the courtyards in 1786 will always be associated with Mozart, Schikaneder and *Die Zauberflöte.*

Left: Mozart's friend and patron, Count Thun, surrounded by the symbols of freemasonry. The emphasis on a secret symbolism did not so much cause the fear of freemasonry as provide a rationalization for that fear. The fear itself was of the liberal and democratic ideas that the freemasons advocated.

Metastasio's old libretto had already been set many times, by Caldara, Leo, Hasse, Gluck, Jommelli and others, but its theme of imperial benevolence had an obvious attraction for the Estates in their pursuit of concessions from Leopold. Since it was more than 50 years old, the libretto was to be modernized, and this task was entrusted to the Dresden court poet Caterino Mazzolà. Presumably Mazzolà was a freemason, for as well as reshaping the structure in the light of subsequent reforms, especially Gluck's, he transformed the Emperor Titus from a Baroque autocrat into an embodiment of masonic virtue. In Mozart's hands, Titus became first cousin to Sarastro, and the score as a whole has much of the simplicity and dignity of his masonic style. The aristocratic audience on 6 September did not much care for it.

There was precious little time for writing this opera. On 26 July Constanze had given birth to her fourth son—Franz Xaver Wolfgang,

one of the two children that survived, the other being Karl Thomas, born in 1784—and barely three weeks later she set out with her husband and Franz Süssmayr on the road to Prague. During the three-day journey, Mozart applied himself intensively, writing both in the coach and at the inns. Süssmayr, a composition pupil who had become a good friend, worked at the *secco* recitatives. Somehow the opera was ready in time, and four days beforehand there was a special performance of *Don Giovanni*, which Mozart seems to have conducted. Given the right stimulus, he still had astonishing reserves of energy. But he was not well in Prague; his friends saw a marked difference in him, especially in his expression when outwardly relaxed, and at the end of the visit he found it hard to say goodbye without uncontrollable tears.

The Mozarts were back in Vienna around the middle of September. Schikaneder was about to present *Die Zauberflöte*, but some of the music

La clemenza di Tito; Carol Neblett as Vitellia and Tatjana Troyanos as Sextus, Salzburg Festival, 1976. The part of Sextus, written for a *castrato*, is now taken by a contralto. Here Vitellia persuades Sextus to fire the Capitol and murder the Emperor Titus (Act I).

Die Zauberflöte, the arrival of Sarastro in his triumphal chariot, drawn by six lions (Act I, Finale); engraving by Joseph and Peter Schaffer, 1793. This is one of a series of engravings thought to have been based on the Freihaus production.

had yet to be written: the composer's catalogue gives 29 September as the date of completion—one day before the first performance. Despite the pressures, these same hectic weeks saw the composition of the Clarinet Concerto (K. 622). Written for Stadler, this is comparable in inventiveness and richness of interplay between soloist and orchestra with the greatest of the piano concertos, and in seriousness it stands alone among the wind concertos. (For all their brilliance and charm, the horn concertos of 1783 and 1786 are diversions by comparison.) In feeling and in treatment, the slow movement of K. 622 is related to the deepest vein in *Die Zauberflöte*, and nowhere is there a hint that the composer was a sick man, still less a dying one.

The first two performances of *Die Zauberflöte* were conducted by Mozart himself, after which the young Johann Henneberg took over. Schikaneder played Papageno's part, and the composer's sister-in-law Josepha Hofer the Queen of the Night: it was an experienced cast and one used to playing to the Freihaus public. On the first night, however,

178

the audience was slow to respond and Mozart had to be reassured by Schikaneder. But the success that followed was overwhelming; during the month of October more than twenty performances were given, and after Mozart's death *Die Zauberflöte* continued to draw full houses. It was lively entertainment, much of the music had that strangely compelling quality which makes people return again and again, and the basic message—the triumph of light over darkness, good over evil—was clear to all. Some, no doubt, were quick to identify the allegorical characters, and soon the inner meaning must have become common knowledge. That a fairy tale can be explosive is effectively shown by Wilfrid Mellers:

Die Zauberflöte, costume design for Papageno, 'the jolly bird-catcher'; engraving by Franz Wolff, Mannheim, 1794. In the original production at the Freihaus Theatre, Vienna, Schikaneder himself played Papageno.

> There are three main strands to Schikaneder's allegory. First there are the Masonic beings who represent Progress and Enlightenment. Tamino is the Emperor Joseph II, Pamina the Austrian people, and Sarastro Ignaz von Born, a Masonic prophet, half rational, half mystical. Then there is the realm of the Queen of Night—what seemed to Masonic enlightenment the effete Catholic world of sorcery, superstition, and seduction. The Queen is Maria Theresa, Monostatos (semi-comic creature of lust and vengeance) is the clergy, and in particular the Jesuits. Finally, there is the world inhabited by those incapable of the heights of humanism: Papageno being, in his innocence, a kind of comic Parsifal.[29]

In the reactionary climate of 1791, when Josephine reforms were being reversed and freemasonry was on the defensive, *Die Zauberflöte* carried with it risks of a kind that was new to Mozart. *Figaro* had necessitated the manipulation of the emperor and his functionaries, nothing more; *Die Zauberflöte* was a standing invitation to the police. Did they have a Mozart file? The notion is neither frivolous nor bizarre. In the light of the subsequent persecutions, of the Illuminati in particular, it is probable that Mozart, had he lived and remained in Vienna, would have gained the attention of the police to an extent that Beethoven never did.

The enthusiasm shown at the Freihaus Theatre was a great consolation to Mozart in the last two months of his life. He was often present at the performances. He fetched young Karl from boarding-school to enable him to see the opera; he took his mother-in-law, and we even find him in a box with Salieri, who 'listened and watched most attentively and from the overture to the last chorus there was not a single number that did not call forth from him a *bravo* or *bello*'.

Mozart's clavichord. Mozart is said to have used this instrument while composing *Die Zauberflöte, La clemenza di Tito* and the Requiem. Acquired by the Mozarteum, Salzburg, on the death of Mozart's younger son, Wolfgang, in 1844.

This glimpse of Mozart and Salieri together is intriguing, for it is almost the only one we have, and it comes at a crucial moment for the legend perpetuated by Pushkin and Rimsky-Korsakov: namely, that Mozart died because Salieri had poisoned him. This is one of a number of fantasies that arose in the wake of Mozart's death and has long since been discredited. Certainly the two men were rivals and viewed each other with suspicion, and there is evidence that Salieri had used his position to try to block *Figaro* and *Don Giovanni*. The poisoning apart, the characterization in Rimsky-Korsakov's opera *Mozart and Salieri* (1897) may not be far wrong. The idea that Salieri was good enough, and serious enough, to *know* that his talent could never match Mozart's genius does make sense. Those who were merely successful careerists— Anfossi, Gazzaniga and the rest—may have disliked Mozart personally but were hardly envious of him; they had no need to be.

During the first half of October, Constanze was at Baden once again. The nature of her ill-health can only be surmised, but there is little doubt that frequent pregnancies were the root of the trouble. After Mozart's death her health improved; she had no children by her second husband, Georg Nikolaus Nissen, whom she married in 1809, and was nearly 80 when she died. To picture her relaxing at Baden while her devoted

180

Wolfgang was becoming more and more gravely ill is perhaps unjust, but some such image is scarcely avoidable. We have no means of telling how aware she was of her husband's condition. When she returned home, however, there was much to make her anxious: fainting fits, an obsession with death, lassitude, sometimes a dejection and mental anguish that made composing impossible. She did what she could, consulting a physician and trying to discourage work on the Requiem.

Desperate attempts to complete the Requiem dominated Mozart's last weeks and days. The mysterious origin of the commission and his own sick state of mind combined to give this work a special significance for the composer. It was his first major work to a liturgical text since the Mass in C minor (K. 427), which he had left unfinished in 1783. In the circumstances, it is pertinent, though largely unavailing, to ask what the liturgy now meant to him. That his view of death had been deeply influenced by masonic thinking is evident from his comments—see, for instance, the letter to his father quoted in Chapter 8—and it is unlikely that this was the only respect in which he had deviated from Catholic orthodoxy. But if any estrangement was involved, it was from the clergy rather than from the Church itself. Like his father before him, Mozart had long been critical of the priesthood, and he must have revelled in the

Die Zauberflöte; Alan Opie as Papageno, John Brecknock as Tamino, Barbara Walker as Pamina, and Neil Warren-Smith as Sarastro, Coliseum, London, 1975. The first performances in England were at the Haymarket Theatre in 1811 and at Covent Garden in 1833.

satirical figure of Monostatos. What the priests thought of Mozart is reflected in the difficulty experienced by Constanze's younger sister, Sophie, in finding one that would come to him when he was dying.

The Requiem is in character partly Catholic, partly masonic. There is much that is deliberately archaic, reminding us of Mozart's enthusiasm for that 'true church music [which] lies in attics, almost eaten by worms'. Sometimes not only the treatment but the actual material is of the high Baroque: for instance, in the fugue (*Kyrie eleison*) which completes the opening number, and in the fugal setting of *Quam olim Abrahae*, of which the falling chromaticism is Bach-like rather than Mozartian. Other things, especially the awesome, majestic music for *Rex tremendae*, actively re-create the Baroque in the manner of the C minor Mass. But there is also the dark-toned, masonic scoring with its emphasis on basset horns, bassoons and trombones, of which the *Maurerische Trauermusik* (K. 477) is the prototype, and there are whole movements that are masonic in style and imagery: the opening *Requiem aeternam*, the luminous *Recordare* with its blend of homophony and a simple polyphony, to say nothing of its ties, suspensions and thirds, and the hymn-like setting of *Hostias*.

When Mozart died, only the first number was complete in every detail, and the last three numbers—*Sanctus*, *Benedictus* and *Agnus Dei*— were non-existent. Of the remaining eight numbers, all but one were complete in essentials, though by no means fully scored. The exception is *Lacrimosa*, which Mozart brooded over on the day before his death: only the first eight bars, including the two of orchestral introduction, are his own composition. In completing the work, Süssmayr presumably followed Mozart's intentions wherever he knew them. According to Constanze, there were some sketches and jottings which she gave to Süssmayr. What those amounted to we do not know; nor do we know the extent to which the two men had discussed the work. From Sophie's account we learn that the completion was discussed within hours of Mozart's death; and yet it was the future court *Kapellmeister* Joseph Eybler that Constanze first asked to carry out this task. There are several imponderables, which is not surprising; Constanze was sick and distraught and for a time took the advice of whoever was at hand. However, that she was capable of trickiness is shown by her pretence that the completed Requiem was entirely the work of her late husband, which it was possible to maintain because Süssmayr's musical handwriting was almost indistinguishable from his.

There is no point in dwelling on the misery of Mozart's last weeks, but certain facts must be set down. For a short time he seemed rather better and on 18 November was able to conduct his newly composed *Kleine*

The dying Mozart, an anonymous nineteenth-century artist's imaginative portrayal. Behind Mozart stands Constanze, and her sister Sophie is at the piano. But there are several respects in which the scene does not bear scrutiny; the impulse behind it is strictly sentimental.

Freimaurer-Kantate (Little Masonic Cantata, K. 623) at the inauguration of a new masonic temple, and he was much gratified by the response. That was a fitting last appearance. Only two days later he became so ill that he had to go to bed. His hands and feet were swollen, he had difficulty in moving, and there were severe bouts of vomiting. He grew rapidly weaker, and the immediate cause of death may have been dropsy rather than uraemia. At the beginning of December there was one more brief improvement; he even spoke of going again to *Die Zauberflöte*. Whenever his head was clear enough, he tried to work at the Requiem. It is said that on the afternoon of 4 December he sang through some numbers from the Requiem with three friends; but later that day he became unconscious. According to Sophie, one of his last requests was that Constanze should tell no one of his death until she had informed Johann Albrechtsberger, whom he regarded as the rightful successor to his expectations at St Stephen's. That was done, and Albrechtsberger, remembered today as one of the teachers of Beethoven, did become the cathedral *Kapellmeister*. Mozart did not regain consciousness. He died shortly before one o'clock the following morning. Both Constanze and Sophie were with him.

What followed has been romanticized by over-zealous Mozartians. The notion of 'a pauper's funeral' appeals strongly to those who wish to shed enjoyable tears, but strictly it is not quite true. The facts of the case are bleak enough and are plainly stated by the Viennese social historian Ilsa Barea:

> Mozart died in a mean two-roomed flat [in the Rauhenstein-gasse] on 5 December 1791 . . . and was taken to St. Marx Cemetery in a third-class funeral (cost eight florins fifty-six kreutzer paid to the parish priest of St. Stephen) against the blast of wind and sleet that made the few mourners turn back at the city gate and leave the light coffin on the hearse (cost three florins) to hired men, to a priest at the graveside, and to a grave-digger who had no duty to mark the spot if no one else did.[30]

That was on 7 December. The mourners included Swieten, Salieri, Albrechtsberger, Süssmayr and probably Hofer and Lange, Mozart's brothers-in-law. Constanze was too ill to be present. Swieten had taken charge, and it was he who arranged the third-class funeral. The rebuke that he could easily have paid for something better has often been made, but this takes into account neither the prevailing social climate nor masonic thinking. It was not an age of sumptuous burials. Indeed, during the Josephine era such 'superstitious' practices were actively discouraged; for a time it was decreed that coffins be abandoned in favour of sacks and quicklime, and a number of ceremonies were abolished. Masonic thinking was similarly opposed to the exploitation of death by the priests. That Constanze made no attempt to find the grave until 1808 may seem more remarkable, but this, too, is in keeping with the age.

Swieten helped to organize a benefit concert, which raised enough money to pay off all Mozart's debts: that is, rather more than 3000 gulden. One would dearly like to know who was present—more than that, who paid conscience money—for the sum is impressive, a sizable contribution from the emperor notwithstanding. Certainly this event, which took place on 28 December, should be set against the doleful story of the funeral. On 11 December, Leopold II had received Constanze and had accepted her petition for a pension. When the bureaucracy had done its work, what she received—just over 266 gulden—was strictly a third of Mozart's meagre salary as court composer. Ilsa Barea notes that, at about the same time, the widow of a Swiss silk manufacturer who had set up a factory in Vienna was accorded a pension of twice that sum.

No wonder that Constanze tried to get all she could from the sale of manuscripts. To describe her behaviour as mercenary, as some have done, is surely perverse. She was only 28, in poor health and had two sons to look after. Moreover, in the event, she remained a widow—nominally, at least—for 18 years. The mercenary note is provided by that same Count Deym who had commissioned pieces for a mechanical organ. As soon as he knew that Mozart was dead, he came to the flat and made a death mask. A little later, one more figure was added to his display of waxworks: Mozart in his own clothes!

MOZART AND OURSELVES

Every age has its own relationship with the great music of the past. Performers and listeners alike tend to emphasize the qualities most at one with their inner needs and predilections. This does not mean that other qualities go completely unperceived, though in extreme cases such a blindness is bound to arise: for example, the flexibility and *espressivo* of the Romantic era argues an unawareness of, or indifference to, the qualities of movement inherent in Baroque and Classical music. Nor does it follow that all ages have distorting mirrors of similar sizes: there is no doubt that the music of J. S. Bach, for example, is far less 'distorted' today than it was 50 years ago. This is only partly a matter of scholarly 'authenticity': that is to say, the correct resources, instrumentally and numerically, and a respect for Bach's performing tradition. It is also a matter of feeling: a desire for the equivalent of a cleaned painting, which is one of our own predilections. And so a Bach chorale is seldom heavily solemnized in the manner that was favoured even 30 years ago.

That some very different sounds have been made in Bach's name is well known. For one thing, the rehabilitation of the harpsichord and other Baroque instruments has taken place within living memory, as has the virtual abandonment of such practices as playing the Third Brandenburg Concerto on the full strings of a symphony orchestra. That Mozart has likewise been subject to different approaches, which means different views of what his music essentially is, is less widely appreciated. This has been touched on in Chapters 8 and 9, and the present vogue for 'chamber' performances of the piano concertos directed from the keyboard is surely a reminder. With Mozart, however, such differences

Die Entführung aus dem Serail; Susan Belling as Blonde, and Herbert Beattie as Osmin, San Francisco, 1968. For a contrast in atmosphere and 'feeling' see p. 189.

have less to do with the resources used and considerably more with the informing spirit. To us, maybe, he has always been there as a model of Classical balance and proportion, but in fact no composer, not even Bach, has undergone more far-reaching changes of emphasis.

So far as the larger part of his music is concerned, Mozart has by no means 'always been there'. Throughout much of the nineteenth century the works that were widely disseminated were neither numerous nor a truly representative cross-section. Most piano students encountered movements from the sonatas, good chamber music players knew and valued the quartets dedicated to Haydn and some other works, and in the concert hall a small selection of piano concertos and symphonies was generally known. This applies to the German lands, central Europe, Scandinavia, England and possibly France; in Italy the picture is still more sketchy. Particularly striking is the lack of interest shown throughout Italy in the operas; to the Italians, Rossini, not Mozart, was the crowning glory of *opera buffa*, and for some time most opera publics north of the Alps were of much the same persuasion.

The fate of the operas is instructive. *Die Zauberflöte* soon became established in German opera-houses, where it acquired a special reputation as the forerunner and inspiration of a number of operas by the first-generation Romantic composers. Moreover, it was revered by Beethoven, who was unsympathetic to the Italian operas on account of their subjects, which he considered unworthy, even immoral. Outside Germany, *Die Zauberflöte* had little real success except in England, but later in the century English audiences generally encountered an almost unintelligible Italian version. (Despite O'Reilly's interest in 1790, it appears that no Mozart opera was given in London until 1811.) *Figaro* and *Don Giovanni* were performed extensively; in Germany, however, they became repertory operas only in German versions with spoken dialogue in place of the recitatives. As 'grand opera' increasingly dominated nineteenth-century taste, so these same two works, wherever they were given, were coloured by an operatic tradition far removed from their own essential spirit. *Così fan tutte* disappeared almost entirely, though for a time, early in the century, gratuitous English 'adaptations' enjoyed some success in London. Not until the Mozart festivals at Munich in the 1890s is there evidence of the kind of responsibility to the operas that we now take for granted.[31]

Those grey facts make salutary reading. The public situation, however, is not the only dimension. Throughout the century there were many dedicated Mozartians, some of them scholarly as well as imaginative. The first big landmarks in Mozart scholarship are the three-volume biography by Otto Jahn and the chronological catalogue of

works compiled by Ludwig von Köchel. These appeared in 1856–9 and 1862. The only earlier biographical essays of importance are the short life (1798) by Franz Niemetschek, of the University of Prague, and the comprehensive biography (1828) by Georg Nikolaus Nissen. (Nissen became Constanze's second husband in 1809 after some years as her lodger and friend: his book was a retirement project completed in Salzburg between 1821 and 1826. Niemetschek was one of Mozart's circle of friends and admirers in Prague, and it was in his household that the two sons, Karl and Franz, received their education.) The foremost examples of individual perception and dedication are the great composers of the century for whom Mozart had a special place. Beginning with Haydn, these include such different creative personalities as Chopin, Brahms, Tchaikovsky, Strauss and Nielsen, to say nothing of Beethoven and Schubert.

Haydn's whole-hearted admiration was exceptional for a musician of his generation. That he felt strongly about the lack of response that he saw around him is amply demonstrated by a letter written in 1787 to a cultivated amateur who had expressed enthusiasm for *Don Giovanni*:

Die Entführung aus dem Serail in its Italian version, *Il Seraglio*; an artist's impression of the closing scene, Drury Lane, London, 1854, drawn for the *Illustrated London News*. From left to right: Pedrillo, Blonde, Osmin, Pasha Selim, Constanze and Belmonte. The first London production was in English in 1827.

For if I could convince every music lover—and especially those in high positions—of the inimitable works of Mozart; if they would judge them, as I do, seriously and with musical understanding; if they would let his music touch their souls as it does my own—why, then the nations would compete with one another for possession of such a jewel within their borders. . . . I am furious that this unique Mozart has not yet been taken into the service of an imperial or royal court.[32]

Uniqueness, seriousness, a capacity for moving deeply: the very qualities rejected by those who complained of 'more genius than taste'. This complaint was made again and again in the notices of Mozart's music from the 'Haydn' quartets onwards, but after Mozart's death it was stood on its head by the Romantic generation represented by E. T. A. Hoffmann, for whom imaginative genius was the highest justification.

Hoffmann was a writer as well as a composer, and it was from the leading writers of the German Romantic movement—for example, Ludwig Tieck, the brothers Schlegel, Hoffmann himself—that a new and positive appraisal of Mozart derived its impetus. Clearly, their Mozart was not the same as Haydn's; their writings suggest a response less balanced, less comprehensive, but undoubtedly intense. They took what they needed: 'Mozart strives for the superhuman and the miraculous that dwell in the depths of the mind'; his music is 'the mysterious language of a distant spiritual kingdom, whose marvellous accents echo in our inner being and arouse a higher, intensive life' (Hoffmann).

Those of Hoffmann's generation who were most active in the cause greatly exaggerated Mozart's affinity with themselves, but they brought new lustre to his name and ensured repeated performances of certain of his works. About Beethoven, however, they were even more enthusiastic, and this resulted in a view of Mozart seen through Beethovenian spectacles of their own making. By concentrating on those of Mozart's works felt to be akin to the 'sublime' and the 'demonic' in Beethoven—for instance, the D minor Piano Concerto and *Don Giovanni*—they fostered a tendency to Beethovenize which persisted in varying degrees throughout the century.

If the Romantic approach implied a rescuing of Mozart from the world of the *ancien régime*, then the other notable tendency in the nineteenth century was to 're-create' him in just such a world. In circles where the arts were regarded as an elegant and stable shelter from the harsher realities of social change, a charming, Rococo Mozart—a figure of Dresden china prettiness—had a natural appeal. If anything, this

Antonio Tamburini as Don Giovanni, Paris, 1841. Tamburini (1800–1876) was the most celebrated operatic baritone of his generation; he first appeared in London in 1832.

shallow, artificial view persisted longer than the Romantic Mozart, for it was not incompatible with the later, more severe doctrine of 'perfection of form'. In the anti-Romantic climate of the early twentieth century, a corrective emphasis on Mozart as form emerged strongly. This came about partly as a result of wider cultural changes, particularly after World War I, but it drew support from a rapidly growing body of Mozart scholarship—the monumental work on the earlier years by Théodore de Wyzewa and Georges de Saint-Foix (1912–45) looms largest—and from a more sophisticated approach to musical history. No longer was it possible to treat Mozart and Haydn as the 'precursors' of Beethoven; their music had come to be seen as an achievement in itself, whatever its place in the continuing stream. This new historical sense had far-reaching consequences, especially for the music of earlier periods, and it meant that even the slightest piece by Mozart could be accepted in its own right.

There is something to be learnt from each of these views. Even the Rococo 'image' can make a contribution, for it depends entirely on an awareness of precise, polished workmanship. Besides, Mozart began within a Rococo culture, which he served with an impeccable sense of style. However, when we talk of style, we often deceive ourselves: we use the term to embrace expression, or simply as a synonym for expression. This is where the Romantics offer a fundamental insight, for the truth that they recognized, and extravagantly exploited, is that the artifice of stylistic convention may be the bearer of a distinctive, even profound, expressive content. In other words, the style is the clothing rather than the man: in Mozart, of all composers, the difference in level is crucial, and at times fathomless. From the Romantics we also get a heightened sense of change and development, albeit coloured by their too-easy assumptions as to where Mozart was heading.

What, then, is the particular emphasis, and bias, of our own age? Probably it is Mozart's complexity, especially psychological complexity. Lacking clear creative convictions, we are unlikely to 'load' the music as heavily as the Romantics. Our self-doubt, reinforced by our historical predilections, encourages the belief that nothing is as simple as it seems; or rather, that such seemings necessarily have many facets. This approach is well represented by Donald Mitchell:

> ... what amazes, and sometimes confuses, is Mozart's mercurial synthesizing, his fleet passing from one mood to another: what one might call his essential ambiguity. How often do we find ourselves confronted with a movement whose character defies verbal analysis, whose content

Die Zauberflöte; above the Queen of the Night, design by Simon Quaglio, Munich, 1818; *below* design by David Hockney for Act II, Scene 8, Glyndebourne, Sussex, 1978. Two contrasting idioms, but each creates a sense of mystery and magic.

challenges our sensibility, the quality of our responses, at their very deepest level, where emotions are not distinct or defined, but partake one of another—which are, as it were, nameless? Mozart sounds, in its double sense, what cannot be named, those deep recesses of the human spirit where opposites are identical, where joy is grief, comedy is tragedy, and laughter another way of weeping—or *vice versa*, if you wish it. Paradox is a prime constituent of the human personality and of the world we live in; it is one of the mainsprings of Mozart's art.[33]

To an age that is surer of itself, this approach will perhaps seem over-subtle, over-sophisticated, but it undoubtedly embodies genuine insights. While something of it takes us back as far as Hoffmann—Mozart sounding 'those deep recesses of the human spirit . . .'—the emphasis, the prominence given to paradox, and in the background the critical scrutiny of musical experience, these are all modern. This kind of perception has added richness and depth to inherited notions of formal perfection. It is seldom today that we hear self-consciously restrained, 'formalistic' performances of the sort that used to be offered, and even acclaimed, in the name of stylistic truth. Such distancing and supposed objectivity has been overcome by our feeling of closeness to Mozart's humanity. In other words, our intuitive responses have proved stronger than the narrower type of historicism.

It is worth pondering how little ground has been gained by the idea of restoring to Mozart the instruments for which he wrote. Performances using a Mozart piano have remained curiosities, and it seems that, for the most part, musicians and music-lovers alike do not desire otherwise. Since the modern concert grand is a very different instrument, both in quality of tone and in weight of tone, we have a situation in which our standards for Mozart differ from our standards for Bach. It might be argued that this is only temporary, and that a time will come when the early piano is as unremarkable for the music of Mozart as is the harpsichord today for the music of Bach.

The analogy with Bach may at first seem persuasive, but it disregards the gulf that separates the Classical from the Baroque. This is best understood subjectively, by reference to our experience of the music, though it can also be expressed in terms of musical techniques. The quality described by Mitchell as Mozart's 'essential ambiguity' has an immediate bearing, for it is the multiplicity of feeling—the experience of contrasts, conflicts, contradictions—that brings the Classical composers so close to ourselves. The Baroque world of absolutes is quite another matter, and our relationship with it is, comparatively speaking, that of outsiders. In stepping back, as it were, however easily and unconsciously, into another culture, we find that our historical selves have come to be sticklers for adherence to the letter: cornetts, shawms and crumhorns are the order of the day. And rightly so; we are dependent on the letter for a rediscovery of the spirit. (Significantly, the quarterly journal *Early Music* includes the Baroque within its scope.)

It is one of the best-kept secrets of musical history that the emergence of the Classical outlook—see Chapter 7—marks a turning-point more decisive than the dawn of Romanticism: that is to say, the crucial change came before Beethoven rather than after. Once grasped, however, this perspective shows clearly why period instruments are irrelevant to our relationship with Mozart. There is nothing 'early' about Mozart; his emotional complexity is ours too, and to that extent we know him for a 'modern'. We also have the advantage of better insights into the nature of the Classical style than have usually been available. The most important of these, and one that embraces many others, is an active, dynamic view of Classical forms, or rather, of the form-making process. The concept of a *process*, sustained by a 'current' that generates tensions at a number of levels, is really quite different from that of a *pattern*. By directing us to the fundamental *movement* of the music, this helps us to see the error in both formalistic pattern-making and Romantic *espressivo*: not for nothing do we speak of the 'movements' of a symphony, concerto or string quartet; and yet, when we are conscious of the term, we tend to associate it with tempo, which is not the same thing. Tempo is pace; movement is something more like pulse, which implies a rhythmical tension and buoyancy. Once sensitive to this quality, we can often tell within the first few bars whether or not a Mozart performance is going to be resilient, alive, consistent and whole.

Consistency is itself one of the canons of our time: consistency in phrase-making and dynamics, and especially a consistent tempo. The conductor or soloist who disrupts the tempo at the behest of spontaneous 'feeling' is sure to be rapped by the critics. Are such canons merely 'of our time' and as certain to be swept away as the foibles of the past? Or dare we suppose that our view of Mozart is more rounded, more comprehensive and therefore more enduring than that of any previous age?

Such heady questions invite headstrong answers. History assures us that the twenty-first century will have its own view of Mozart, but it does not follow necessarily that that view will differ radically from our own. Subjective needs are modified by objective knowledge, and it is surely neither headstrong nor 'the arrogance of the present' to suggest that our legacy of knowledge and experience of Mozart's music will be

formidable. To put it another way: given our immense advantages, if we have not reached a point at which Mozart can be seen more or less whole, then we ought to have done!

Advantages, it is said, carry disadvantages on their backs, and in one respect this may well be applicable to Mozart and ourselves. It concerns the problem of over-familiarity. Performances of some of Mozart's greatest works—the last three symphonies, for instance—have become so 'everyday' that, as listeners, we may easily slip into a too-familiar response. We are lulled by the certainty of what comes next and our listening ceases to be active. The best corrective is to widen our scope, to make a point of experiencing some of the unfamiliar works. These, in turn, will provide fresh insights. Readers might like to take stock of the works mentioned in this book, noting which are familiar and which are not: recordings of nearly all are currently available. A discussion of many more is to be found in Einstein's *Mozart, his Character, his Work*, which remains the most rewarding single volume on the subject.

Die Zauberflöte, Act I, Finale; Tamino charms the wild beasts with his flute—the aria 'Wie stark ist nicht dein Zauberton' (O voice of magic melody). Two conceptions of naturalistic fantasy: *right* engraving by Ramberg, early nineteenth century, and *above* Joseph Köstlinger as Tamino with a walrus at his feet, film production by Ingmar Bergman, 1975.

196

NOTES

Chapter 1: Salzburg and the Mozart Family

1 Eric Blom, *Mozart*, Dent, (rev. edn) London 1952; Octagon Books, New York 1947.
2 *ibid*.
3 The extracts from Mozart's letters and from those of members of his family are given in Emily Anderson's translation: see *The Letters of Mozart and his Family*, Macmillan, London 1938, 1966. There are three exceptions, all in Chapter 4: the postscript by Anna Maria and one sentence from a letter by Wolfgang are from Erich Schenk, *Mozart and his Times*, Secker & Warburg, London 1960; the extract from a letter written by Leopold in February 1771 is from Arthur Hutchings, *Mozart*, Thames & Hudson, London 1976; Schirmer Books, New York 1976.

Chapter 2: The Child Prodigy

4 Daines Barrington, 'Account of a Very Remarkable Young Musician', in *Philosophical Transactions of the Royal Society*, vol. lx, 1770.
5 An influential literary journal published in Paris, 1747–90. In the 1760s, Melchior Grimm was the editor. Quoted in Schenk, *op. cit*.

Chapter 3: Early Compositions

6 'My Prince was always satisfied with my works. Not only did I have the encouragement of constant approval, but as conductor of an orchestra I could experiment, observe what produced an effect and what weakened it, and was thus in a position to improve, to alter, make additions and omissions, and be as bold as I pleased. I was cut off from the world; there was no one to confuse or torment me, and I was forced to become original.' Haydn on his position as *Kapellmeister* to Prince Nicholas Esterházy: see Karl Geiringer, *Haydn, A Creative Life in Music*, Allen & Unwin, London 1947; University of California Press, Berkley 1968.
7 Jens Peter Larsen, 'The Symphonies', in H. C. Robbins Landon and Donald Mitchell (eds.), *The Mozart Companion*, Faber & Faber, London 1965; Norton, New York 1970.
8 Alfred Einstein, *Mozart, his Character, his Work*, Cassell, (2nd edn) London 1956; Oxford University Press, New York 1965; repr. Panther, London 1977; the source for all references to Einstein.
9 Quoted by Gerhard Brunner in the programme-book for the Salzburg Festival, 1971. Chrysander wrote extensively on *Mitridate* in the *Allgemeine musikalische Zeitung* (Vienna), 1881–2.
10 Edward J. Dent, *Mozart's Operas*, Oxford University Press (2nd edn.), London and New York 1947. For the operas, see also William Mann, *The Operas of Mozart*, Cassell, London 1977; Oxford University Press, New York 1976.

Chapter 4: A New Order in Salzburg

11 Hutchings *op. cit*.
12 In his *Deutsche Chronik*: quoted in Schenk, *op. cit*.

Chapter 5: The Developing Composer

13 An inheritance from the Baroque—see, for instance, the fugue in E major from Book II of Bach's 48 Preludes and Fugues. This first figures prominently in Mozart's music in the *Credo* of the Mass in F major (K. 192); it consists of the notes 1, 2, 4, 3—in C Major, C, D, F, E.
14 See Katharine Thomson, *The Masonic Thread in Mozart*, Lawrence & Wishart, London 1977: the source for all references to Thomson.
15 Dent, *op. cit*.: the source for all references to Dent.

Chapter 6: Vienna: Mozart turns Freelance

16 See Schenk, *op. cit*.

Chapter 7: Mozart and Haydn

17 Vincent and Mary Novello (ed. Medici and

Hughes), *A Mozart Pilgrimage*, Eulenburg, London 1975.

18 Quoted in Max Graf, *Composer and Critic*, Chapman & Hall, London 1947; well worth referring to for reactions to Mozart in his own time.

19 Donald Francis Tovey; see especially his *Essays in Musical Analysis*, Oxford University Press, 1936, 1972, for many insights into the Classical style. See also Charles Rosen, *The Classical Style*, Faber, 1971; indispensable for anyone wishing to study in depth.

Chapter 8: Operatic Masterpieces

20 This, for example: 'Nobility, fortune, rank, position! How proud they make a man feel! What have *you* done to deserve such advantages? Put yourself to the trouble of being born—nothing more! For the rest—a very ordinary man! Whereas I, lost among the obscure crowd, have had to display more knowledge, more calculation and skill merely to survive than has sufficed to rule all the provinces of Spain for a century!' Trans. John Wood, Penguin, 1964.

21 Michael Kelly (ed. Fiske), *Reminiscences*, Oxford University Press, 1974.

Chapter 9: Piano Concertos and String Quintets

22 See Thomson, *op. cit.*, chapters 13 and 15.

23 Hutchings, *op. cit.*; see also his *Companion to Mozart's Piano Concertos*, Oxford University Press, 1950.

24 Wilfrid Mellers, *The Sonata Principle* (*Man and his Music*, vol. 3), Rockliff, London 1957; repr. Barrie & Jenkins, London 1969.

Chapter 10: Poverty and Riches

25 'The number three has a special significance in Freemasonry.' ... 'the radiant *Allegro* opens with a theme consisting of a rising chord of E flat and a major sixth, expressing hope and joy. In the second subject pairs of slurred quavers denote the ties of brotherhood.' Thomson, *op. cit.*

26 The question of musical and expressive unity is too complex to be discussed here. Readers who wish to look into this should refer to the fascinating analysis in Deryck Cooke, *The Language of Music*, Oxford University Press, 1959.

27 Richard Strauss (ed. Schuh, trans. Lawrence), *Recollections and Reflections*, Boosey & Hawkes, London 1953.

Chapter 11: The Last Twelve Months

28 See Ilsa Barea, *Vienna, Legend and Reality*, Secker & Warburg, 1966, pp. 89ff.

29 Mellers, *op. cit.*, p. 153. Mellers is following Moritz Alexander Zille, whose commentary on *Die Zauberflöte* was published anonymously at Leipzig in 1866.

30 Barea, *op. cit.* Even this account has been challenged. A. Hyatt King refers to 'the mild and misty weather prevailing at the time' and remarks that the mourners would not have accompanied the hearse 'because funeral processions were then forbidden by law on grounds of public health'—see his *Mozart*, Bingley, London 1970, pp. 7–8.

Chapter 12: Mozart and Ourselves

31 Dent, *op. cit.*, is my principal source. In the preface to the second edition he notes that when his book was first published (1913) 'most of Mozart's operas were almost completely unknown' in England.

32 Quoted by Friedrich Blume, in Robbins Landon and Mitchell (eds.), *op. cit.*

33 See Robbins Landon and Mitchell (eds.), *op. cit.*, Foreword, p. xii.

CHRONOLOGY

1756   Wolfgang Amadeus Mozart born at Salzburg, 27 January.

1761   First compositions: short keyboard pieces written down by Leopold Mozart.

1762   Two exploratory concert tours: to Munich (January) and Vienna (September–December).

1763   Leopold appointed vice-*Kapellmeister* at Salzburg. The 'grand tour' begins (June): Munich, Augsburg, Ludwigsburg, Schwetzingen, Mainz, Frankfurt, Coblenz, Aix-la-Chapelle, Brussels, Paris, Versailles.

1764   In London (April): meets J. C. Bach and composes first symphonies.

1765   Departure from London (July). At The Hague gravely ill with typhus.

1766   Return journey: Amsterdam, Paris, Dijon, Lyons, Geneva, Lausanne, Berne, Zurich, Munich, Salzburg (November).

1767   Second visit to Vienna (September). Very ill with smallpox.

1768   In Vienna: composes *La finta semplice* and the *Waisenhausmesse*.

1769   Returns to Salzburg (January). Italian tour begins (December).

1770   Verona, Mantua, Milan, Bologna, Florence, Rome, Naples. Receives Order of the Golden Spur from Clement XIV. Lessons from Martini. *Mitridate* produced in Milan (December).

1771   Returns to Salzburg (March). To Milan (August) for production of *Ascanio in Alba* (October).

1772   Colloredo succeeds Schrattenbach as Archbishop of Salzburg. Mozart appointed *Konzertmeister* (August). To Milan (October) for production of *Lucio Silla* (December).

1773   Third visit to Vienna (July–September). Six string quartets (K. 168–73). Symphony in G minor (K. 183).

1775   *La finta giardiniera* produced in Munich (January). Five violin concertos (K. 207, 211, 216, 218, 219).

1776   *Serenata notturna*. Deepening antipathy between Colloredo and the Mozarts.

1777   Piano Concerto in E flat (K. 271). To Munich (September) with Anna Maria; then to Augsburg and Mannheim. Falls in love with Aloysia Weber.

1778   In Paris (March–September). Anna Maria dies. *Paris* Symphony.

1779   Reluctantly returns to Salzburg (January) and re-enters the archbishop's service as court organist. *Coronation* Mass. Sinfonia Concertante in E flat (K. 364).

1780   Mass in C (K. 337). Symphony in C (K. 338). To Munich (November) to complete *Idomeneo*.

1781   Production of *Idomeneo* in Munich (January). Summoned to join Colloredo's entourage in Vienna (March), where he is dismissed (May). Meets Constanze Weber and becomes engaged.

1782   Freelance in Vienna. Production of *Die Entführung aus dem Serail* (July). *Haffner* Symphony. Serenade in C minor (K. 388). Marries Constanze (August). Piano Concertos (K. 413–15). First 'Haydn' Quartet (K. 387).

1783   Birth and death of first son. Takes Constanze to Salzburg and returns via Linz. Mass in C minor (K. 427). *Linz* Symphony.

1784   Second son, Karl Thomas, born. Piano Concertos (K. 449–51, 453, 456, 459). Becomes a freemason (December).

1785   Leopold visits Vienna. 'Haydn' Quartets completed. Piano Concerto in D minor (K. 466).

1786   Production of *Le nozze di Figaro* (May). Birth and death of third son. Piano Concertos in A (K. 488), C minor (K. 491) and C major (K. 503). *Prague* Symphony.

1787   Leopold dies. First daughter born (dies 1788). Two visits to Prague (January, September). *Don Giovanni* produced in Prague (October). String Quintets in C (K. 515) and G minor (K. 516). Appointed chamber composer by Joseph II. Decline in health begins.

1788 Increasing financial difficulty: begins borrowing from Puchberg and others. Last three symphonies, in E flat (K. 543), G minor (K. 550) and C (K. 551).

1789 Visits Dresden, Leipzig, Berlin. Returns to Vienna via Prague (May). First 'Prussian' Quartet (K. 575). Clarinet Quintet (K. 581). Constanze's first 'cure' in Baden. Birth and death of second daughter.

1790 Production of *Così fan tutte* (January). Visits Frankfurt at time of imperial coronation of Leopold II (October). String Quintet in D (K. 593).

1791 Fourth son, Franz Xaver, born. To Prague for production of *La clemenza di Tito* (September). *Die Zauberflöte* produced in Vienna (September). Piano Concerto in B flat (K. 595). String Quintet in E flat (K. 614). Clarinet Concerto (K. 622). Requiem (K. 626) left unfinished. Mozart dies, 5 December.

GLOSSARY

Adagio (*It.*) slow—appreciably slower than *andante*; particularly associated with Beethoven's slow movements.

Allegretto (*It.*) moderately quick, but slower than *allegro*.

Allegro (*It.*) lively—indicates a fairly quick time.

Andante (*It.*) literally, at a walking pace—a very moderate time, slower than *moderato*.

Antiphon a piece of church music in which one voice (priest) and many voices, or two groups of voices, sing alternately.

Aria (*It.*) air, song, especially in opera and oratorio; *da capo* aria, one in three sections, the third being a repeat of the first, often with embellishments.

Baroque originally a term pertaining to architecture—elaborate, ornate, bizarre; now applied to the arts in general, and particularly to the culture of the courts, in the period *c.* 1600–1750.

Basset horn a type of alto clarinet in F with a richer, more sombre tone; particularly associated with Mozart's masonic music.

Bravura (*It.*) literally, bravery—technical brilliance and display; a *bravura* passage, one demanding virtuosity.

Cadence-figure a short melodic idea used in making a cadence—the close of a musical phrase, 'sentence' or 'paragraph'.

Canon (*It.*) literally, according to strict rule—a strict form of counterpoint in which one part is exactly and regularly imitated by one or more others.

Cantata (*It.*) literally, a sung composition—a choral work designed in a number of movements, usually with orchestral accompaniment.

Cantata mass a setting of the mass in which each section of the text is divided musically into several movements, in the manner of a cantata.

Cantabile (*It.*) in a singing style.

Canzonetta (*It.*) literally, little song—in an *opera buffa* a popular song, usually in 6/8 time.

Castrato (*It.*) literally, castrated—the male soprano voice of the seventeenth and eighteenth centuries for which many of the most important parts in *opera seria* were written; also found in the choirs of Roman Catholic cathedrals and chapels.

Chromaticism the use of notes outside the prevailing diatonic (major or minor) scale: for example, in C major, the black notes of the piano.

Clavier (*Fr., Ger.*) literally, keyboard—a term applied to various keyboard instruments, but especially the harpsichord and the piano.

Coda (*It.*) literally, tail—the closing 'paragraph' of a musical form; *codetta*, a little coda, as at the end of the exposition section in a sonata form.

Coloratura (*It.*) a florid, virtuosic vocal style, especially in Italian opera.

Commedia dell' arte (*It.*) the traditional Italian popular comedy with the figures of Harlequin, Columbine,

Pantaloon, etc. and extemporized dialogue; a form of 'licensed jesting', sometimes uproariously scornful of authority.

Concertante (*It.*) concerto-like, soloistic.

Concerto (*It.*) a composition for one or more solo instruments and orchestra.

Concerto grosso (*It.*) literally, great concerto—from Corelli onwards, the foremost Baroque orchestral form, usually contrasting a small group of instruments (*concertino*) with the main body (*ripieno*).

Continuo (*It.*) an abbreviation of *basso continuo*, a type of bass part in Baroque music from which a keyboard player is required to extemporize the correct harmonies.

Contrabasso (*It.*) double-bass—abbreviated Cb. or C.B.

Contredanse (*Fr.*) country dance.

Corno (It.) horn—abbreviated Cor.

Counterpoint the interaction of two or more simultaneous melodic parts.

Divertimento (*It.*) an instrumental composition in several movements (often five or six) intended to divert; the *cassation* and serenade are also of this type.

Dominant seventh the chord formed on the dominant (fifth degree) of any scale and consisting of the major triad with the addition of the minor seventh: for example, in the key of C, the notes G B D F—such a chord seeks 'resolution' on the tonic chord, in this case C E G.

Ensemble (*Fr.*) literally, together—has several uses, one meaning an operatic number for several of the principals: for example, a trio or quartet.

Espressivo (*It.*) literally, with expression—when used pejoratively, with an excess of expression.

Fagotto (*It.*) bassoon—abbreviated Fag.

Fantasia (*It.*) fantasy—a composition in free form.

Festa teatrale (*It.*) literally, theatrical festival—a festive opera in celebration of a special occasion.

Fugue a highly developed type of contrapuntal composition characterized by the successive entries of the parts in imitation.

Grotesco (*It.*) an acrobatic clown.

Homophony music that is conceived vertically, in chords, with one predominant part (melody) to which the others furnish harmonies, as opposed to polyphony.

Larghetto (*It.*) a little *largo*—a slow time, but not as slow as *largo*.

Libretto (*It.*) literally, booklet—an opera text.

Major key a key whose common chord consists of the key-note, the major third and the perfect fifth—in C major, C E G.

Minor key a key whose common chord consists of the key-note, the minor third and the perfect fifth—in C minor, C E-flat G.

Minuet dance in triple time, French in origin, but in the eighteenth century fashionable throughout Europe.

Missa brevis (*Lat.*—pl. *missae breves*), a concise setting of the text of the mass, without musical elaboration.

Motet a choral composition, normally for use in church but to a non-liturgical text.

Opera buffa (*It.*) the eighteenth-century Italian comic opera, popular in spirit and much given to social satire, however lightly.

Opera seria (*It.*) literally, serious opera—the eighteenth-century Italian tragic opera, characterized by plots drawn from ancient history or mythology, elaborate staging and much formality; outside Italy essentially the opera of the courts.

Operetta (*It.*) little opera—a light opera.

Opus (*Lat.*) a work. Opus numbers are useful in referring to particular compositions, especially when there are no distinctive titles.

Oratorio a dramatic composition for concert performance (not staged), usually to a religious text.

Overture a self-contained orchestral introduction to an opera, oratorio or ballet.

Part an individual line or strand in a composition; for example, an oboe part, or a soprano part.

Part-writing the lay-out of a composition in respect of the quality of its individual parts.

Polyphony music that is conceived horizontally, in three or more simultaneous melodic parts, as opposed to homophony.

Quadrille a kind of country dance.

Recitative a voice part intended to be sung in a speech-like manner; used for narration in opera and oratorio, and generally followed by an aria.

Ritornello (*It.*) literally, little return—a short instrumental or orchestral passage that recurs between the verses of a song or between the 'solos' in a concerto.

Rococo the decorative dissolution of the Baroque; a culture of extreme refinement, elegance and stylized sentiment, preoccupied with its own exquisiteness.

Rondo (*It.*) a musical form in which the principal theme (and key) regularly recurs, alternating with other themes.

Scena (*It.*) literally, scene—a dramatic composition for solo voice and orchestra, usually consisting of a recitative and aria.

Secco recitative 'dry' recitative (*It.*)—recitative accompanied only by a few chords from a keyboard instrument, usually a harpsichord.

Sequence the repetition of a phrase at a higher or lower pitch.

Serenata (*It.*) serenade; also denotes a type of cantata, usually pastoral in character, popular in the eighteenth century.

Sinfonia (*It.*) symphony—originally used to describe any purely orchestral number in an opera, oratorio, etc., and especially the overture: for example, the 'Pastoral Symphony' in Handel's *Messiah*.

Sinfonia concertante (*It.*) a hybrid musical form, basically symphonic but with two or more solo instruments, as in a *concerto grosso*.

Singspiel (*Ger.*) a play with singing, an operetta—usually denotes an eighteenth-century popular opera with spoken dialogue, the German equivalent of the French *opéra comique* and the English ballad opera.

Sonata (*It.*) a composition for one or two instruments (or more, in rare cases), usually in three or four movements.

Sonata form see Preface.

Sonata-rondo a musical form combining the characteristic features of sonata form and rondo.

Style galant (*Fr.*) a term used in reference to musical style in the period of transition from Baroque to Classical; may often be interpreted as the Rococo in music, but also applied to early expressions of the emerging Classical outlook—see the beginning of Chapter 3.

Symphony the characteristic orchestral form of the Classical period: at first in three movements, extending the three sections (quick, slow, quick) of the Italian operatic overture (*sinfonia*), but later with the addition of a minuet before the finale.

Tempo (*It.*) time—the pace at which music moves.

Time-signature an indication of measure and beat: for example, 4/4 means four crotchets in a bar (two groups of two), 6/8 six quavers in a bar (two groups of three).

Triplet a group of three notes within the time accorded by the time-signature to two (or four) of the same value: for example, three quavers in place of two.

Tutti (*It.*) all the performers—denotes a passage in which the whole orchestra is playing, as distinct from more thinly scored passages.

BIBLIOGRAPHY

Anderson, Emily (ed.), *The Letters of Mozart and his Family*, Macmillan, London 1938, 1966.

Barea, Ilsa, *Vienna, Legend and Reality*, Secker & Warburg, London 1966.

Blom, Eric, *Mozart*, Octagon Books, New York 1949; Dent (rev. edn.), London 1974.

Brophy, Brigid, *Mozart the Dramatist*, Faber & Faber, London 1964; Harcourt Brace Jovanovich, New York 1964.

Burney, Charles (ed. Scholes), *Musical Tours in Europe*, Oxford University Press, London 1959.

Carse, Adam, *The Orchestra in the Eighteenth Century*, Heffer, Cambridge 1940.

Cooke, Deryck, *The Language of Music*, Oxford University Press, London 1960.

Dent, Edward J., *Mozart's Operas*, Oxford University Press, London and New York 1947.

Deutsch, Otto Erich, *Mozart: A Documentary Biography*, A. & C. Black, London 1965; Stanford University Press, Stanford, Calif. 1966.

Einstein, Alfred, *Gluck*, J. M. Dent & Sons, London 1936.

Einstein, Alfred, *Mozart, his Character, his Work*, Cassell, (2nd edn) London 1956; Oxford University Press, New York 1965; repr. Panther, London 1977.

Forman, Denis, *Mozart's Concerto Form*, Hart Davis, London 1971.

Geiringer, Karl, *Haydn, A Creative Life in Music*,

Allen & Unwin, London 1947; University of California Press, Berkley 1968

Geiringer, Karl, *The Bach Family*, Allen & Unwin, London 1954; Oxford University Press, New York 1954.

Girdlestone, C. M., *Mozart's Piano Concertos*, Cassell, London 1948.

Graf, Max, *Composer and Critic*, Chapman & Hall, London 1947.

Hutchings, Arthur, *Companion to Mozart's Piano Concertos*, Oxford University Press, London and New York 1950.

Hutchings, Arthur, *Mozart*, Thames & Hudson, London 1976; Schirmer Books, New York 1976.

Jahn, Otto, *Life of Mozart*—3 volumes, (trans. Townsend), E. F. Kalmus, London 1968; Cooper Square, New York 1970.

Kelly, Michael (ed. Fiske), *Reminiscences*, Oxford University Press, London 1974.

King, A. Hyatt, *Mozart Chamber Music*, BBC, London 1968; University of Washington Press, Seattle 1969.

King, A. Hyatt, *Mozart*, Clive Bingley, London 1970.

Landon, H. C. Robbins, *The Symphonies of Joseph Haydn*, Barrie & Jenkins, London 1961.

Landon, H. C. Robbins, *Essays on the Viennese Classical Style*, Barrie & Jenkins, London 1970; Macmillan, New York 1970.

Landon, H. C. Robbins and Mitchell, Donald (eds.), *The Mozart Companion*, Faber & Faber London 1965; Norton, New York 1970.

Lang, Paul Henry, *Music in Western Civilization*, Dent, London 1942.

Mann, William, *The Operas of Mozart*, Oxford

University Press, New York 1976; Cassell, London 1977.

Mellers, Wilfrid, *The Sonata Principle (Man and his Music,* vol. 3), Barrie & Jenkins, London 1969.

Mellers, Wilfrid, *Romanticism and the Twentieth Century (Man and his Music,* vol. 4), Barrie & Jenkins, London 1969.

Novello, Vincent and Mary (ed. Medici and Hughes), *A Mozart Pilgrimage*, Eulenburg, London 1975.

Robinson, Michael F., *Opera before Mozart*, Hutchinson, London 1972.

Rosen, Charles, *The Classical Style*, Faber & Faber, London 1971.

Saint-Foix, Georges de, *The Symphonies of Mozart* (trans. Orrey), Dobson Books, London 1947.

Schenk, Erich, *Mozart and his Times*, Secker & Warburg, London 1960.

Thomson, Katharine, *The Masonic Thread in Mozart*, Lawrence & Wishart, London 1977.

Tovey, Sir Donald Francis, *Symphonies (Essays in Musical Analysis,* vol. 1), Oxford University Press, London 1936, 1972.

Wangermann, Ernst, *From Joseph II to the Jacobin Trials,* Oxford University Press, London and New York 1969.

Wangermann, Ernst, *The Austrian Achievement, 1700–1800*, Thames & Hudson, London 1973; Harcourt Brace Jovanovich, New York 1973.

Wellesz, Egon, and Sternfeld, Frederick (eds.), *The Age of Enlightenment (The New Oxford History of Music*, vol. 7), Oxford University Press, London and New York 1973.

Yorke-Long, Alan, *Music at Court*, Weidenfeld & Nicolson, London 1954.

ACKNOWLEDGEMENTS

We are grateful to the following for the use of illustrations:
Jacket: Scala/Mozart Museum
Back Jacket: Museum Carolino Augusteum, Salzburg

Endpapers: Österreichische Nationalbibliothek

Archiv für Kunst und Geschichte: 2–3, 10, 24, 31, 48, 67, 96, 98, 109, 110, 129, 139, 164; Chris Arthur: 181;

Eric Auerbach: 134; Clive Barda: 72, 132; Bate Collection: 157; British Museum: 63, 86 (top), 103, 144, 152; British Museum/John Freeman: 33, 108; Bulloz: 115, 119; Colt Clavier Collection: 136; Foto Saporetti, Milan: 52; Fotomas Index: 30 (bottom); Gesellschaft der Musikfreunde in Wein: 86 (bottom), 151; Giraudon: 40; Guy Gravett: 154, 192 (bottom); James Heffernan: 173; I.G.D.A./Louvre: 38; Mander and Mitchenson Theatre Collection: 191; Mansell Collection: 44, 89, 95, 149, 183; Mary Evans Picture Library: 60, 189, 197; Museum Carolino Augusteum, Salzburg: 12, 18; Ladislav Neubert: 127; Margaret Norton/*Opera* Magazine: 186; Österreichische Nationalbibliothek: 81, 120, 123, 174, 175, 178; Phonogram Int./Gaston H. Richter: 4; Reproduced by Gracious Permission of Her Majesty the Queen: 32; Royal College of Music: 43, 99, 113, 116, 122, 126; Salzburger Festspiele Pressbüro: 177; Scala: 35 (Mozart Museum), 49, 51 (Mozart Museum), 55 (Louvre), 75 (Museo Teatrale alla Scala), 77 (Museo Civico, Turin), 84, 145, 171 (Mozart Museum); Donald Southern: 101, 165; Staatliche Graphische Sammlung, Munich: 111; Stadtbildstelle Augsburg: 15, 30 (top), 69, 79, 167, 176; Sveriges Radio: 196; Dr J. Svoboda: 131, 161, 163; Theatre Museum, Munich: 130, 179, 192 (top); University of Glasgow: 90; Zefa/Dr K. Biedermann: 85; Zefa/M. Thonig: 13.

We are particularly grateful to the Mozart Museum in Salzburg for their kind co-operation and for providing the following illustrations: 16, 17, 27, 56, 58, 66, 68, 100, 104, 168, 180.

INDEX

Note: references to illustrations are in italics